IMAGES
of America

COVINGTON'S SISTERS OF NOTRE DAME

In this 1928 photograph, 10 young aspirants pose in front of the main entrance to the convent at St. Joseph Heights. Aspirants are young women of high school age who board with the Sisters of Notre Dame at the convent while continuing their education at the academy and evaluating the prospect of religious life. (Courtesy of the Sisters of Notre Dame Archives.)

On the Cover: The members of the Covington Province of the Sisters of Notre Dame pose for a group photograph in front of their St. Joseph Heights Provincial House and Convent in Park Hills, Kentucky. The 1974 photograph was taken as part of the 100-year anniversary of the sisters' immigration to the United States and the Diocese of Covington, Kentucky. (Courtesy of the Sisters of Notre Dame Archives.)

IMAGES
of America

COVINGTON'S SISTERS OF NOTRE DAME

Wm. Michael Hargis

ARCADIA
PUBLISHING

ISBN 978-0-7385-8230-6

Published by Arcadia Publishing
Charleston, South Carolina

Printed in the United States of America

Library of Congress Control Number: 2010940117

For all general information, please contact Arcadia Publishing:
Telephone 843-853-2070
Fax 843-853-0044
E-mail sales@arcadiapublishing.com
For customer service and orders:
Toll-Free 1-888-313-2665

Visit us on the Internet at www.arcadiapublishing.com

I dedicate this book to my mother, Ruth Warken Hargis, a graduate of both Mother of God Elementary School and Notre Dame Academy and a lifelong supporter of the Sisters of Notre Dame.

Contents

ACKNOWLEDGMENTS

As with most endeavors of this nature, this book would not have been possible without the support and encouragement of a large group of individuals and organizations who enthusiastically contributed their photographs, historic information, and guidance to the project. In recognition of their assistance, I wish to acknowledge Mother of God Parish Archives; the Diocese of Covington Archives; the *Messenger* Archives; the Sisters of Notre Dame Archives, Covington Province; Dr. Paul Tenkotte, chairperson of the Department of History and Geography at Northern Kentucky University; photographer Raymond Hadorn; Bishop Brossart High School; and numerous Catholic parishes and organizations.

Sincere thanks goes to Arcadia Publishing for the opportunity, given I am a first time author, and to my editor, Amy Perryman, for her guidance and support.

I would also like to thank my family and friends for their help and encouragement throughout the process of researching and writing this book. A special thanks to my wife, Liz Hargis, for her technical assistance and support over the six months of collecting and organizing the materials for this book.

Lastly, I wish to thank Sr. Mary Joan Terese Niklas, archivist for the Sisters of Notre Dame, Covington Province. Without her dedicated research effort and historical knowledge, this book would not have been possible.

The following is additional information about this book:

The majority of the photographs in this book are the property of the Sisters of Notre Dame Archives. Photographs provided by other sources are credited within the book.

Due to the limitations of space, all of the schools and affiliations of the Sisters of Notre Dame of the Covington Province were not able to be included in this book. Those that have been included are representative of the more than 75 affiliations since 1874.

In 1980, the Sisters of Notre Dame were given the option to change their name back to their baptismal name. Names shown in parentheses represent the sister's name prior to 1980.

INTRODUCTION

The date of October 1, 2010, marked the 160-year anniversary of the founding of the Sisters of Notre Dame in Coesfeld, Germany. It is from these hardy German roots that the Sisters of Notre Dame of the Covington Province can trace their heritage.

In 1848, a 20-year-old teacher at St. Lambert's School in Coesfeld, Germany, agreed to care for an indigent young girl in her home. From that experience, Hilligonde Wolbring realized that she had a calling to care for the orphaned and neglected children of the city. Hilligonde was not alone in this desire to serve. Together with fellow teacher and close friend Elisabeth Kuhling, the two young women began their journey to educate and care for the needy children of Coesfeld.

Having observed the dedication exhibited by the two young teachers, the parish priest at St. Lambert, Fr. Theodore Elting, suggested that the establishment of a formal congregation to provide a sound religious and economic basis would be advisable. After due consideration, Hilligonde and Elisabeth accepted his proposal. Arrangements were made for three sisters from Amersfoort, Holland, to travel to Coesfeld to introduce the German candidates to the spirit of their congregation, which itself was based on that of the Sisters of Notre Dame of Namur, Belgium, founded by St. Julie Billiart in 1804.

Sr. Maria Aloysia (Hilligonde) and Sr. Maria Ignatia (Elisabeth) formally established the Sisters of Notre Dame of Coesfeld, on October 1, 1850. Six years later on October 5, 1856, Mother Maria Anna, from Munster, Germany, was elected unanimously as the first superior general of the Coesfeld congregation.

By 1871, Germany was under the rule of Chancellor Otto von Bismarck and the liberal wing of the German Reich. One of the government's objectives was the secularization of the state and society in general, thus eliminating the influence of religion within Germany and in particular Prussia. The movement was known as the "Kulturkampf." By 1875, laws were enacted to forbid religious congregations from teaching in the schools and accepting new members. All religious foundations were given six months to disband and were ordered out of the country.

With the winds of oppressive political change, came the realization that the survival of the Coesfeld congregation could only be achieved outside the borders of Germany. As a result, Mother Maria Chrysostoma, the second superior general, accepted the invitation of Bishop Richard Gilmour to send six sisters to the Diocese of Cleveland, Ohio, to teach in the parish schools. With this affiliation, the Sisters of Notre Dame would take their first step onto the shores of America and embrace the opportunities that life in the land of freedom would offer.

On June 19, 1874, Mother Maria Chrysostoma, Sr. M. Aloysia, and six other sisters boarded the steamship *Rhein* in Bremen, Germany, for the voyage to the United States and the uncertainty of a future in an unfamiliar land. At the conclusion of a 16-day voyage across the Atlantic Ocean, the ship with the eight Sisters of Notre Dame entered New York Harbor at 4:00 p.m. on Saturday, July 4, 1874. Upon their arrival, the weary travelers accepted the hospitality of the Franciscan Sisters and rested until the evening of the following day and the final leg of their voyage. After an 18-hour train ride, the sisters arrived at Union Depot in Cleveland, Ohio, where two horse-drawn carriages delivered them to the small wood-framed house near St. Peter's Church that would be their first home in America.

Upon hearing of the arrival of the sisters from Coesfeld, Germany, Bishop August Toebbe of the Diocese of Covington, Kentucky, hurriedly traveled to Cleveland in the hope that his natural sister, Sr. M. Modesta, was among the eight recent arrivals. Sadly, she was not, but the bishop did request that two of the sisters be sent to Covington to teach at Mother of God School. Mother M. Chrysostoma graciously granted his request, and two sisters were promised by the start of the coming school year.

By mid-August 1874, Sisters M. Odilia and Ignatia arrived in Covington and immediately began to prepare for their introduction into Mother of God School and Parish. Bishop Toebbe had arranged for the Sisters of Notre Dame to live with the Franciscan Sisters at St. Elizabeth Hospital, which was located on Eleventh Street, until a more convenient location could be provided. In the meantime, this arrangement required the two sisters to walk the five blocks between the school and their residence four times each day in the sweltering summer heat. Within several weeks, Father Teutenberg, pastor of Mother of God Parish, located a house directly behind the school at 516 Montgomery Street. The small two-story brick building was quickly prepared, and the Sisters of Notre Dame were in their new home by the end of September.

Sr. Mary Modesta, the sister of Bishop Toebbe, was among the second group of sisters to arrive in the United States. By the summer of 1875, she and several other sisters were in Covington and living at the house on Montgomery Street. It quickly became apparent that the five-room house was too small to meet their present needs and, most certainly, inadequate for the future. Sr. Mary Modesta immediately embarked on a search for a suitable solution to the problem. In July 1875, she purchased a large 12-room house on Fifth Street between Madison Avenue and Montgomery Street. However, as increasing numbers of sisters continued to come to Covington, this home became inadequate as well. Living conditions became so difficult that a number of the sisters were required to sleep on straw mats on the floor of vacant classrooms at Mother of God School. Adjacent property along Fifth Street was purchased and construction began in the summer of 1875 on a new four-story brick building, Notre Dame Academy. The new academy and convent building was completed within 12 months and dedicated by Bishop Toebbe on July 26, 1876. This new academy and convent would be the hub of activity for the Sisters of Notre Dame for the next 50 years.

Initially, Notre Dame Academy provided kindergarten and elementary school classes for both boys and girls, with a limited curriculum for older children. In 1906, a four-year high school program for girls only was established and experienced rapid growth in its enrollment. By 1938, the two-year commercial program and the elementary grades were discontinued to provide additional space for the rapidly expanding four-year program.

As ever increasing numbers of Sisters of Notre Dame immigrated from Coesfeld, Germany, to America the requests for teachers in the Covington Diocese continued to grow. From their initial affiliation in 1874 at Mother of God School, the sisters' association with a number of additional parish schools began in 1875. The parish schools included St. John (Covington), St. Augustine (Covington), St. Stephen (Newport), St. Augustine (Augusta), and St. John (Carrollton). In 1876, Sacred Heart (Bellevue), St. Mary (Alexandria), and Notre Dame Academy (Covington) were added to the ever-growing list of parish schools being served by the Sisters of Notre Dame. Most of these schools continue to have sisters from the Covington Province on their staffs today.

As early as 1848, Sr. Mary Aloysia, the foundress of the Sisters of Notre Dame of Coesfeld, had held a personal desire to care for orphaned children. In 1877, the Sisters of the Covington Province eagerly accepted the challenge of operating two homes for children. The Sisters of Notre Dame staffed St. Aloysius Orphanage in Bond Hill, Ohio, from 1877 to 2000 and St. Joseph Children's Home in Cold Spring, Kentucky, from 1877 to 1961. In 1957, the Sisters of Notre Dame took charge of St. John's Children's Home in Fort Mitchell, Kentucky. In 1961, the Diocese of Covington merged St. Joseph Children's Home with St. John's Children's Home to form the Diocesan Catholic Children's Home, which is presently located in Fort Mitchell, Kentucky.

As the academy and convent on Fifth Street continued to experience steady growth, the decision was made to search for a rural location that would meet future needs. As a result, in 1907, the Sisters of Notre Dame purchased two properties along Lexington Pike. The first property was made up of six acres, known as Old Fedders Corner (currently Park Hills Animal Hospital), and later in the year, 33.75 acres comprised the second property, the Berry Tract. Initially, the property was to serve as a retreat for the sisters serving in the city classrooms and as a haven for the elderly and ill sisters. The ultimate dream was that the property would some day be the location of a new convent for the Covington District. In order to fully realize their dream, the Sisters of Notre Dame hoped to purchase the adjacent Heck Farm, which was not for sale at the time. The sisters offered daily prayers for their intention and even buried a St. Joseph medal in the ground with the promise that the property, if acquired, would be named after the saint. In 1912, Theodor Heck finally relented and agreed to sell his 14-acre farm to the Sisters of Notre Dame, increasing their total land holdings on the Dixie Highway to 54 acres.

World War I temporarily interrupted the dream of the new convent, since sources of financial support for the project were not available. However, at the conclusion of the war, interest in the project was rekindled. In 1922, John F. Cook, of Cincinnati, organized the St. Joseph Heights Home Association with the primary objective of raising adequate funds for the construction and debt retirement of the new convent. The primary fundraising activities of the association were the July 4 Festival and the Autumn Kermess.

The annual July 4 Festival at St. Joseph Heights proved to be a highly successful fundraising event and became one of Northern Kentucky's most anticipated social gatherings each summer. With the help of hundreds of volunteers, the festival attracted thousands of people who were entertained by vaudeville acts, donkey races, boxing bouts, and style shows. It is recorded in the festival annals that in 1932, a parachute jumper was paid $1.50 to leap from the highest point of the convent's roof to the amazement of the excited crowd below. The festival patrons were served chicken dinners for 50¢ and were encouraged to participate in the major raffle for prizes, such as new automobiles and new houses.

The Kermess was a four-day event held each year in November. This became another successful source of funds for the convent project. In 1940, three thousand two hundred turkey and frog leg dinners were served over the four days. In 1937, it is recorded that the turkeys served at the Kermess were actually raised by the sisters on the property of St. Joseph Heights.

Within four years of establishing the St. Joseph Height Home Association, their fundraising activities would allow the construction to begin on the new convent at St. Joseph Heights. On September 12, 1926, the cornerstone was laid, and just over a year later on November 6, 1927, Bishop Francis Howard dedicated the new convent, with over 6,000 supporters in attendance.

A milestone event in the history of the Covington Province occurred in 1924. The newly elected Superior General Mother Mary Cecilia visited the Covington District and announced that on March 12, 1924, Rome had declared that Covington was to be established as a province for the Sisters of Notre Dame. Mother Mary Cecilia also announced that Sr. Mary Angela would be the new superior of the Covington Province.

Notre Dame Academy remained on Fifth Street in Covington after the Provincial House was relocated to St. Joseph Heights. However, with an ever increasing enrollment and the financial burden of maintaining the outdated and rapidly deteriorating facilities, it was determined that the academy should be relocated. To this end, Sr. Mary Agnetis was asked to search for a wealthy benefactor who would support the new academy project with a major financial commitment. After years with no success, on March 1, 1955, Sr. M. Agnetis sent the legendary letter of appeal to Conrad Hilton requesting his financial assistance. The uniquely worded letter gained the interest of the hotel magnate and resulted in a 1956 visit to St. Joseph Heights, where Hilton toured the proposed site for the new academy. Shortly after his visit, Hilton indicated his support for the project by making a pledge of $500,000. Additional funds were raised locally, and on April 16, 1961, ground was broken for the new Notre Dame Academy on Hilton Drive. The first classes were held in the new facility on October 28, 1963. The academy's facilities have undergone a number of renovations and additions since 1963. In 2009, the most recent building campaign was completed with the addition of a performing arts center, new athletic fields, and classroom renovations.

The old Notre Dame Academy facilities on Fifth Street in downtown Covington were sold shortly after the move to the new academy was complete. All of the buildings were demolished in 1964, except for the chapel, which served as office space for the property's new owner, Howard Adams Automobile Dealership. In 1995, the property was purchased by the General Service Administration and is the location of the new federal courthouse. The chapel was demolished, but the facing of the cornerstone is currently displayed at Notre Dame Academy on Hilton Drive, and the 1901 time capsule with contents is preserved at the Archives of the Covington Province.

The Covington Province has a 60-year history of operating medical and senior care facilities. In 1950, the Sisters of Notre Dame purchased their first hospital in the United States when they acquired the buildings and equipment for the Lynch, Kentucky, hospital from the United States Steel Company for $1. The facility was renamed Notre Dame Hospital and served its Appalachian residents until 1961. At the request of the Diocese of Covington, the Covington Province opened St. Charles Care Center in Covington, Kentucky, in 1961, and in 1963, the St. Claire Medical Center was opened in Morehead, Kentucky.

In recent years, the Sisters of the Covington Province have ventured into a variety of additional service ministries. In 1995, the mission in Buseesa, Uganda, East Africa was established, and today, it includes an elementary school, high school, farm, and convent with 11 Sisters of Notre Dame of Covington, Kentucky, serving the residents of the region. In 2010, the latest ministry was implemented with the opening of the Notre Dame Urban Education Center in downtown Covington. This after-school program was designed to provide one-on-one tutoring opportunities for inner-city students as a means of assisting them in reaching their full academic and personal potential.

Since their arrival in Covington in 1874, the Sisters of Notre Dame have served in approximately 70 venues, including elementary schools, high schools, colleges, hospitals, senior care centers, orphanages, child care facilities, medical research laboratories, domestic services in seminaries, a foreign mission, and an urban education center. Through their dedicated services and unassuming spirit, the Sisters of Notre Dame of the Covington Province have touched the lives of hundreds of thousands of people and have made our world a better place in which to live. The legacy of the two young schoolteachers who established the Sisters of Notre Dame of Coesfeld continues to live on in the Sisters of Notre Dame of Covington.

One

Hands across the Sea

The coat of arms is symbolic of the history of the Sisters of Notre Dame and their devotion to Our Lady, the Blessed Virgin Mary. The star of the sea represents *Notre Dame* (Our Lady). The central cross with large roundel represents the center of the Coesfeld congregation in Rome. The five small roundels symbolize France, which is where St. Julie Billiart founded the Sisters of Notre Dame. The lion represents both Belgium and the Netherlands, while the eagle is symbolic of Germany and the founding of the Sisters of Notre Dame of Coesfeld. The lily represents Mary Immaculate, who is the patroness of the United States. The quotation below reads as follows: "Dei Gloria Mariae Honor, for the Glory of God, the Honor of Mary."

St. Julie Billiart was born in Cuvilly, France, in 1751 and founded the Sisters of Notre Dame de Namur in 1804. She became the spiritual mother of a number of religious congregations, including the Sisters of Notre Dame of Amersfoort, Netherlands, and Coesfeld, Germany. St. Julie dedicated her life to educating poor and destitute young girls of the inner city. She died on April 8, 1816, and was canonized on June 22, 1969. St. Julie's feast day is celebrated each year on May 13. (Courtesy of author.)

The Sisters of Notre Dame of Amersfoort, Netherlands, were instrumental in the education of the Coesfeld congregation according to the spirit of St. Julie Billiart. This c. 1850 photograph shows a group of Amersfoort novices and their directresses. The professed sister seated in the center is Sr. M. Brigitte Hans, who was the first novice directress for the Sisters of Notre Dame of Coesfeld.

This uniquely designed Coesfeld crucifix hangs in St. Lambert Church in Coesfeld, Germany. Created by an unknown artist around 1250 AD, it was in front of this cross that Hilligonde Wolbring and Elisabeth Kuhling made the life-changing decision to dedicate themselves to helping the poor. Their decision ultimately gave birth to the Sisters of Notre Dame of Coesfeld.

Sr. M. Aloysia, Hilligonde Wolbring, is the foundress of the Sisters of Notre Dame of Coesfeld. She was born in 1828 and grew up in the Netherlands. She was trained in the methods of Bernard Overberg at the Royal Teacher Training Seminar in Munster and began her teaching career at St. Lambert Parish in Coesfeld, Westphalia. Hilligonde and her teacher friend Elisabeth Kuhling felt a calling to help the poor and indigent children of the city. Answering this calling, the two friends became foundress and co-foundress of the Sisters of Notre Dame of Coesfeld in 1850. Sr. M. Aloysia was a member of the first group of sisters to travel to the United States. She died in 1889 and is buried at St. Joseph Cemetery, Cleveland, Ohio.

Sr. M. Ignatia, Elisabeth Kuhling, is the co-foundress of the Sisters of Notre Dame of Coesfeld. She was born in Munster in 1822 and graduated from the Royal Teacher Training Seminar for Women in 1840. She then taught the older girls at St. Lambert Parish in Coesfeld. In 1850, she joined her friend Hilligonde Wolbring in founding the Sisters of Notre Dame of Coesfeld. Sr. M. Ignatia died from cancer at the age of 47 in 1869.

St. Lambert Church and School are depicted in this artist's drawing. It was in the small building on the right that Sr. M. Aloysia taught the younger children, while Sr. M. Ignatia taught the older girls in the larger building on the left.

Fr. Theodore Elting was the parish priest at St. Lambert Parish, where he also taught religion to the schoolchildren. Born in 1819, Father Elting became acquainted with the dedication and loving care that Hilligonde and Elisabeth showed to the children in their charge. It was at Father Elting's suggestion that the two women were encouraged to continue their ministry to the poor children through the formation of a religious congregation. Father Elting became the first spiritual director of the Sisters of Notre Dame of Coesfeld. He died at the age of 43 in 1862.

It was in a similar house on this lot at 42 Suring Street in Coesfeld that Hilligonde and Elisabeth began their care for neglected children. In October 1849, the two friends moved into the house along with seven young indigent girls. Hilligonde, whose mother and father had died when she was a child, donated her entire inheritance of 10,000 thaler to the new endeavor.

St. Annathal was an abandoned former convent, when, in 1850, Father Elting was able to acquire the building and renovate it to serve as the new home for the newly formed Sisters of Notre Dame and the children in their care. The building first served as home for orphans and neglected children and later a boarding school for girls. St. Annathal became the first motherhouse of the Sisters of Notre Dame of Coesfeld.

Mother Maria Chrysostoma was the second superior general of the Sisters of Notre Dame of Coesfeld. She held this office from 1872 through 1895. It was under Mother Chrysostoma's leadership that the decision was made to send six sisters to the United States to serve in the Diocese of Cleveland, Ohio, in 1874.

This is an artist's depiction of the SS *Rhein*. The ship brought the first Coesfeld sisters to the United States in the summer of 1874. The ship carrying Mother M. Chrysostoma, Sr. M. Aloysia, and six other sisters departed Bremerhaven at 11:00 a.m. on June 19, 1874, and arrived in New York on July 4, 1874.

The first convent house of the Sisters of Notre Dame of Coesfeld was located in St. Peter's Parish in Cleveland, Ohio. The sisters arrived by train from New York at twilight on July 6, 1874.

Bishop August Maria Toebbe served as the bishop of Covington, Kentucky, from 1872 through 1884. On hearing of the sisters' arrival, Bishop Toebbe traveled to the Cleveland convent to see if his natural sister, Sr. M. Modesta, was among the new arrivals. While disappointed that she was not, Bishop Toebbe requested that two of the sisters be sent to Covington to teach at Mother of God School. His request was granted, and two sisters arrived in Covington on August 15, 1874. (Courtesy of Mother of God Archives.)

Mother of God Church and Rectory are seen in this mid-19th century photograph. The first parish school was a single-story brick building, located on the lot directly behind the church. (Courtesy of Mother of God Archives.)

Fr. Peter Teutenberg was the second pastor of Mother of God Parish in Covington, Kentucky. Serving from 1872 until 1879, Father Teutenberg was pastor when the Sisters of Notre Dame arrived in Covington in August 1874. He was instrumental in helping the Sisters of Notre Dame establish themselves in the parish and school. (Courtesy of Mother of God Archives.)

The first convent was located in this two-story brick house at 516 Montgomery Street in Covington. The five-room structure housed three teachers and a housekeeper. As additional sisters arrived from Germany, the house could not accommodate everyone, and as a result, a number of the sisters had to sleep on straw bedding on the floor of the school's classrooms.

The second school to be constructed by Mother of God Parish was located across the street from the church on a lot adjacent to the firehouse. The three-story brick building was constructed by Anton Bley and served as the girls' school upon completion in 1857. (Courtesy of Mother of God Archives.)

These Mother of God schoolgirls pose with their unidentified teacher in this c. 1900 photograph. The location of the photograph is believed to be in the courtyard of the girls' school, which was next to the firehouse on Sixth Street in Covington. (Courtesy of Mother of God Archives.)

Sr. M. Modesta was the newly named superior of the American Foundation and the natural sister of Bishop August Toebbe. Upon her arrival in Covington in 1875, she immediately determined that a new convent was required if future growth was to be realized. Property on Fifth Street, between Madison Avenue and Montgomery Street, was purchased, and construction was begun on a new four-story convent and academy by the fall of 1875.

On August 13, 1905, Bishop Camillus Maes officiated at the laying of the cornerstone for the new Mother of God School on Sixth Street. It was a day of great celebration, and a crowd of more than 10,000 people attended the ceremony. (Courtesy of Mother of God Archives.)

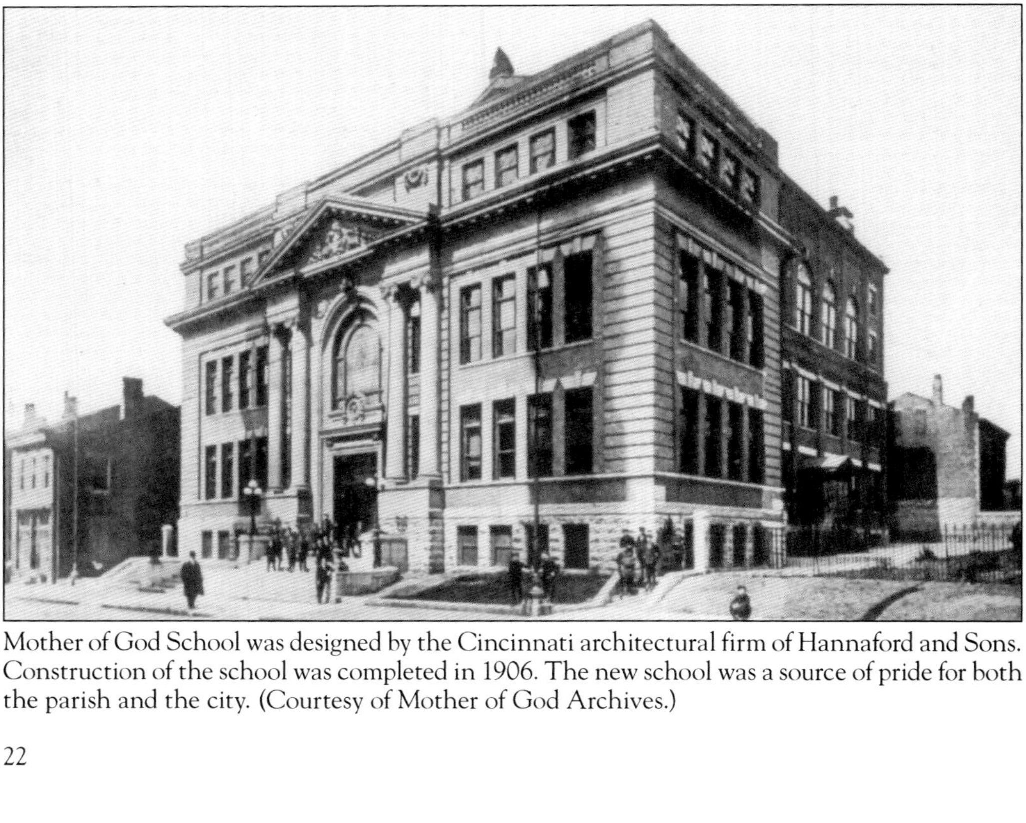

Mother of God School was designed by the Cincinnati architectural firm of Hannaford and Sons. Construction of the school was completed in 1906. The new school was a source of pride for both the parish and the city. (Courtesy of Mother of God Archives.)

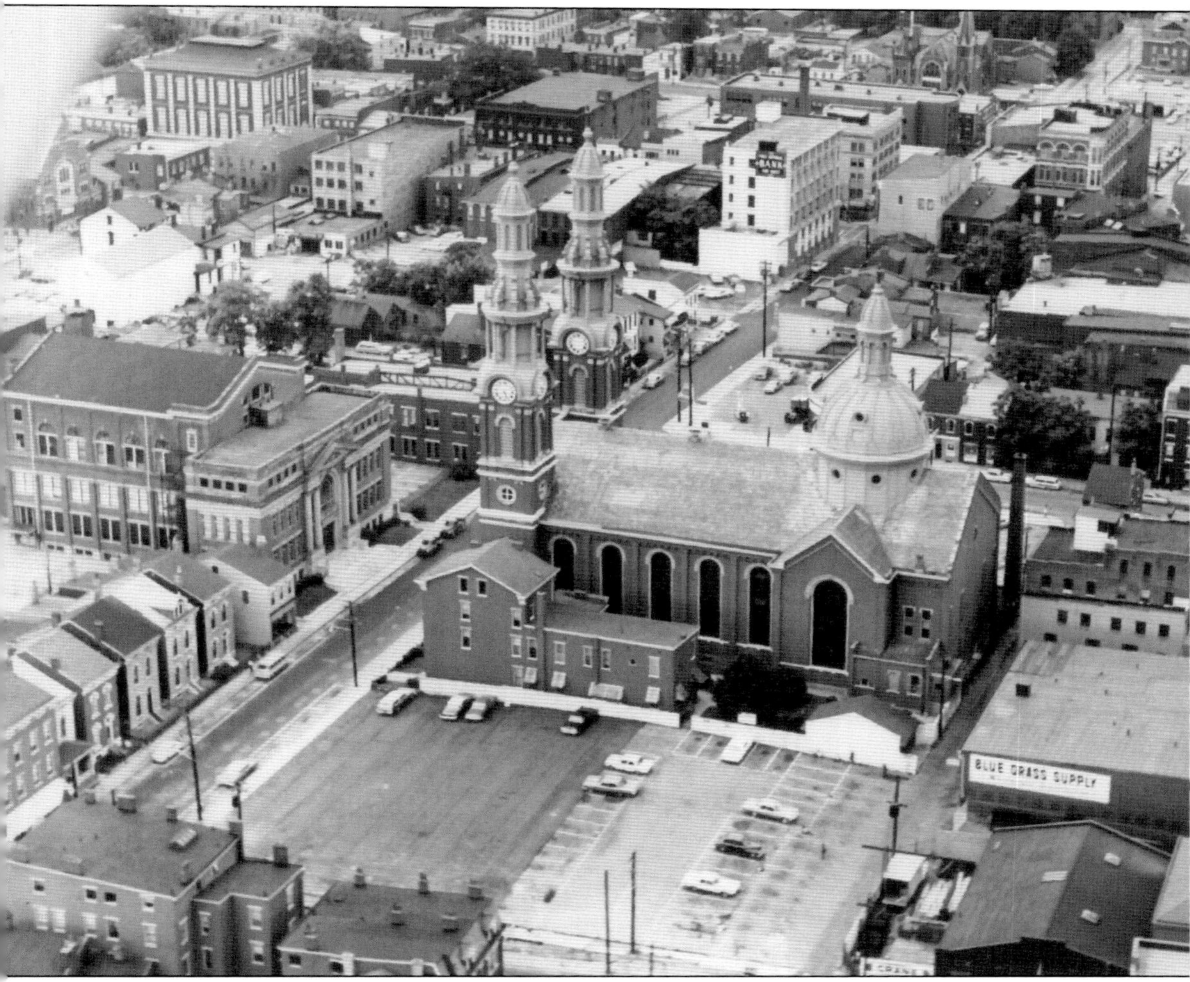

This 1965 aerial photograph shows the relationship of the new school to Mother of God Church and Rectory across Sixth Street. Also seen is the vacant lot on which the girls' school had stood between the new school and the firehouse.

This 1940s photograph of the front elevation of Mother of God School depicts the Classical detailing employed at the main entrance of the building. The school was considered a renaissance in educational design in its day. The design accommodated an auditorium, gymnasium, cafeteria, music room, recreation rooms, and classrooms. (Courtesy of Mother of God Archives.)

Two

Old Notre Dame Academy

A visit to the Covington convent by Mother M. Cecilia, seen in the first row at center, provided the opportunity for becoming more closely acquainted with the new novices of the district. This 1924 visit was also an occasion for celebration, as Mother M. Cecilia announced that Covington was to become the newest province, an independent administrative entity that reports directly to the superior general in Rome, of the Sisters of Notre Dame of Coesfeld.

Since its dedication on July 26, 1876, the Sisters of Notre Dame Convent and Academy in Covington has seen thousands of local citizens and their children cross the threshold of this simple, yet finely detailed, entrance in search of Catholic education and spiritual solitude.

Notre Dame Academy and Convent on Fifth Street was located on the full block from Madison Avenue to Montgomery Street. The original four-story building was completed in 1876, and subsequent additions were added in 1895 and 1897 to accommodate the rapid increase in the academy's enrollment.

This photograph of the Notre Dame Academy Chapel was taken around 1940 and shows the remodeled sanctuary and altar. An interesting observation is that the statues of the Blessed Mother and St. Joseph were relocated to opposite sides of the altar from their location in the original chapel.

In 1924, the members of the Sisters of Notre Dame gathered at the convent on Fifth Street to celebrate the naming of Covington as the newest province. Making the announcement, pictured

in the first row and fifth from the right, is Mother M. Cecilia, the superior general of the Sisters of Notre Dame.

This photograph, taken around 1900, shows the boys and girls of one of the younger classes at Notre Dame Academy. Prior to 1906, the academy provided classes for children in the elementary grades, as well as older children at the high school level.

Five young girls play on the maypole, as three others patiently watch the fun. This early-1900 photograph also shows the tennis court at Notre Dame Academy in the background.

Young girls from Notre Dame Academy grade school are dressed in their finest white dresses for this early-1900s photograph. The occasion and location of the photograph are unknown.

Student cast members from Notre Dame Academy School of Music pose in their variety show costumes worn for the 1934 performance of *Mother Goose Musical*. The school instructors in charge of this production were Srs. M. Erma and M. St. Clare.

Notre Dame Academy students are pictured in the chemistry lab in this 1920s photograph. The polished wooden lab table and glass-fronted shelving units enhanced the simplicity of the room. A single incandescent fixture hanging above the lab table provided illumination.

As shown in this c. 1920 photograph, the sewing classroom was the center of interest for many of the young academy women. Students work with sewing machines along the wall, while the more detailed hand stitching is practiced at the tables in the center. A dress fitting is in progress in the rear of the room.

The bookkeeping class in this early-1930s photograph was instructed on the proper techniques of accounting and record filing as part of their educational program. The academy offered a two-year commercial program until 1934, at which time the curriculum was discontinued to make room for the four-year program.

Physical activities and sports were an integral part of the Notre Dame Academy experience. In this early-1900s photograph, several young ladies take advantage of the tennis court located in Devou Park.

The young ladies of Notre Dame Academy have worn many variations of school uniforms over the years. This fashionable one-piece, loose-fitting dress with contrasting neck scarf was the style of choice in the 1920s.

The 1930s brought a new look to the academy's formal school uniform. This one-piece navy blue dress, with belted waist, decorative buttons, and pleated front, presented a more formal look. Gold and blue capes were worn for special occasions, including graduation. An example of this uniform is in the care of the Archives at St. Joseph Heights Convent.

Two academy students work on their porcelain painting projects during art class in this 1920s photograph. Watercolor and oil painting classes were also very popular with many of the young ladies.

The academy's student newspaper staff is shown working on the latest edition of the *Gavel* in this c. 1910 photograph. It is interesting to see the vintage typewriter being used, as well as the desk lamp that is plugged into the overhead light fixture.

As Notre Dame Academy and Convent continued to see steady growth, it became necessary to search for expansion opportunities. In 1921, this two-story residence immediately east of the main building was purchased and became the Notre Dame School of Music. The second floor was eventually dedicated to the academy's fine arts program.

This 1920s interior view of the Notre Dame Academy Music School Building shows the residential character of the instruction areas and a number of the musical instruments available to the students.

Three academy students stop to discuss the day's events in this early-1950s photograph. The two young ladies on the right entered the Notre Dame Convent after graduation and are identified as, from left to right, Srs. M. Ann Christine and M. Claire.

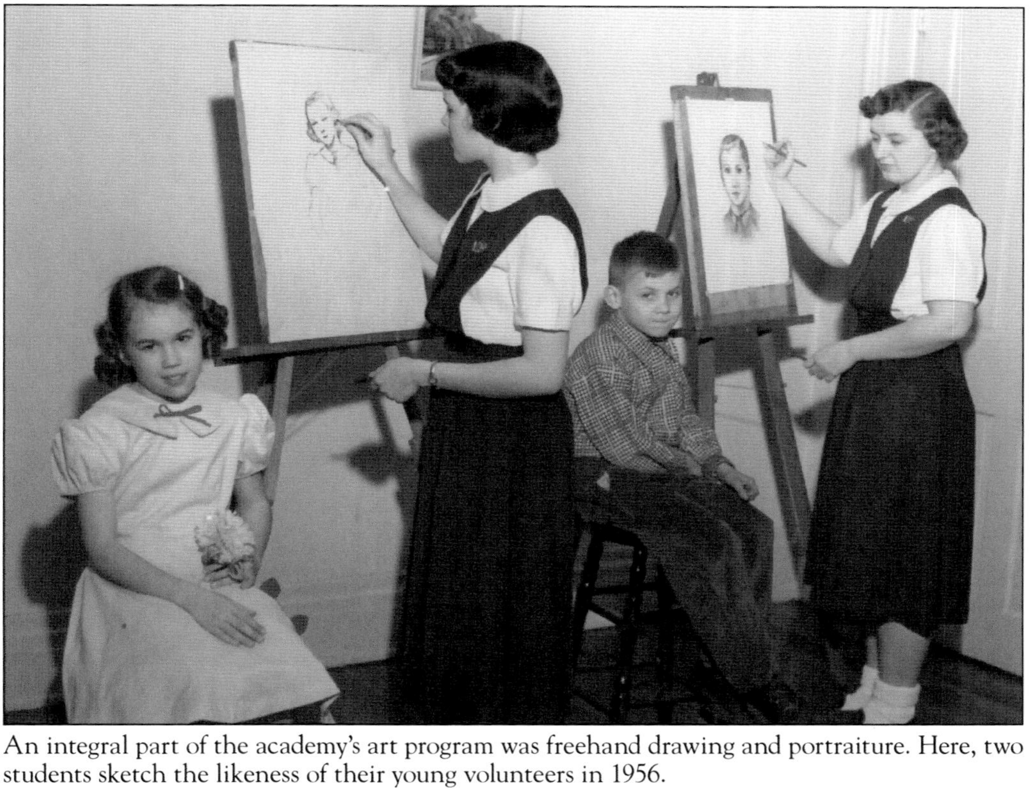

An integral part of the academy's art program was freehand drawing and portraiture. Here, two students sketch the likeness of their young volunteers in 1956.

This early-1930s photograph, which was taken on Fifth Street in front of the Music School Building, shows the student body of Notre Dame Academy. It is estimated that 175 students attended the academy at the time of this photograph.

Classes are out for the day, as students pose in front of Notre Dame Academy and their homebound buses in this c. 1955 photograph. (Courtesy of Raymond Hadorn.)

Three

St. Joseph Heights

This beautifully sculpted statue of St. Joseph, holding the child Jesus lovingly in his arms, stands prominently at the end of the main entrance drive in front of St. Joseph Heights Convent. Mrs. Charles Trame presented the statue as a gift to the Sisters of Notre Dame in the 1930s. (Courtesy of author.)

The first convent at St. Joseph Heights was located in this small brick house out on a six-acre farm on the Lexington Pike. Originally known as the Old Fedders Corner, the property was purchased in 1907 for $3,975. Besides the farmhouse, the property included stalls for cows, horses, and pigs, as well as a large poultry yard. Today, this property is the home of the Park Hills Animal Hospital. (Courtesy of author.)

This weathered iron cross measuring 3.25-by-1.75 inches was discovered on the grounds of the original convent in 1986. Estimated to be approximately 100-years-old, the cherished relic is now located in the convent's archives.

This aerial view of the St. Joseph Heights property shows the extent of the land purchased from 1907 to 1912. In all, a total of 54 acres was accumulated over a seven-year period at a total cost of $42,945. Some of the property, including the original convent, was eventually sold to allow the residential development along St. Joseph Lane, as shown above left.

Mother M. Cecilia was the third superior general of the Sisters of Notre Dame of Coesfeld, serving from 1895 to 1925. It was under her leadership that the sisters in Covington were encouraged to acquire the property and construct the new convent at St. Joseph Heights.

In October 1922, John F. Cook and his Knights of Columbus colleagues, of Price Hill, organized the St. Joseph Heights Home Association. Their avowed purpose was to secure the required funds to construct the new convent on the grounds of St. Joseph Heights. After four years of their dedicated effort and the support of all the local cities in the vicinity, their goal was realized and construction of the convent was approved.

Construction started in the summer of 1926, and the cornerstone for the new Provincial House was laid on September 12 of that year. By the following fall, the new convent was completed, and on November 6, 1927, the facility was open for public inspection.

A group of novices enjoys an afternoon excursion on the lake behind the convent in this c. 1930 photograph. The lake was located in the area of the present-day parking lot for Notre Dame Academy.

Mother M. Angela, the first provincial superior (right), and Sr. M. Ignace, the provincial secretary, pose in front of the lake at St. Joseph Heights in this c. 1930 photograph. After a severe rainstorm in 1933, the lake disappeared, leaving only a large valley behind the convent.

After the acquisition of the St. Joseph Heights property in 1912, one of the first orders of business was to renovate the existing barn into a small chapel, as seen in this c. 1920 photograph.

The year 1927 saw not only the completion of the convent but also the elegant chapel. The interior design of the new chapel is very similar to that of the old chapel at Notre Dame in Covington. On December 24, 1927, the installation of the chapel pews was completed at noon, and the following morning, a festive Christmas worship service was offered.

The most visually stimulating feature of the convent's chapel is the vibrantly colored stained glass windows lining the side walls. Designed by the F.X. Zettler Company in Munich, Bavaria, there are nine large windows and two smaller windows in the main chapel. (Courtesy of author.)

Two smaller stained glass windows can be found standing side by side in the chapel's choir loft. Each of these windows depicts a musician with their respective instrument. Another four small windows are located high in the sanctuary. (Courtesy of author.)

The total cost of all 14 windows in 1927 was $5,650. This included shipping from Germany, import duties, and installation. While historically priceless to the Sisters of Notre Dame, the conservative value of the windows today would be in the hundreds of thousands of dollars. (Courtesy of author.)

The wooden bridge depicted in this c. 1930 photograph was located along the lower end of the lake and connected the convent to the former location of the Shrine of Our Lady of Lourdes.

A group of five novices visits the new Shrine of Our Lady of Lourdes, located on the northeast end of the convent's grounds. The shrine was erected in 1976 and includes two white carrara marble statues that were donated by Clara Archinger.

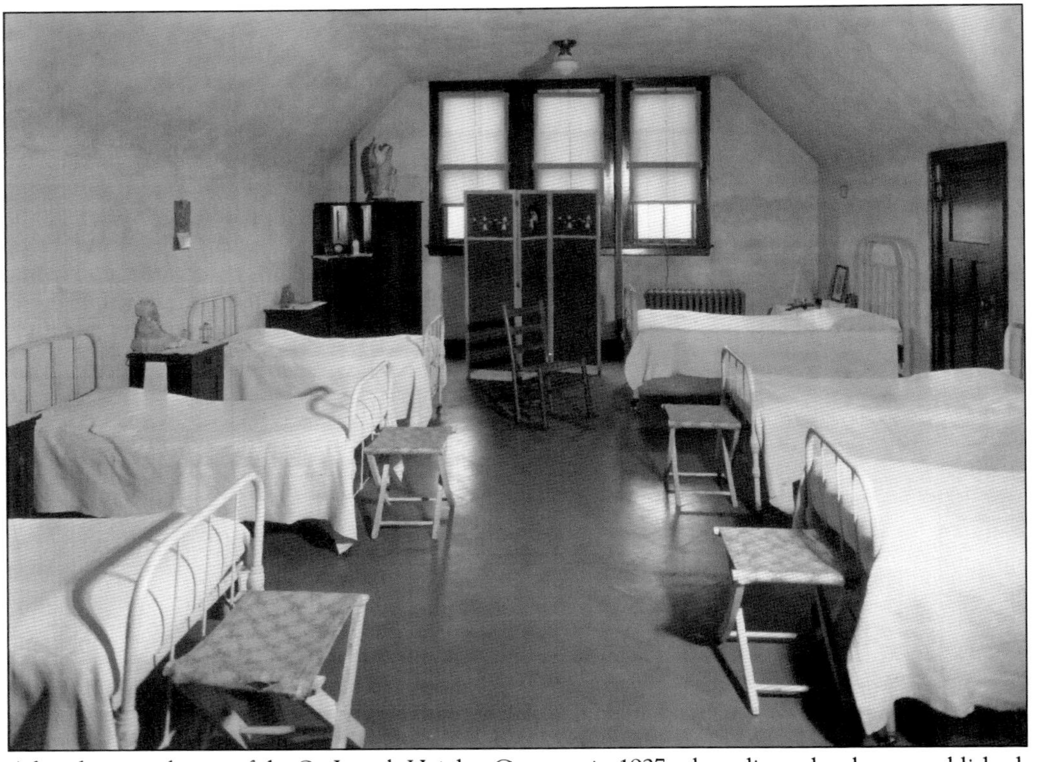

After the completion of the St. Joseph Heights Convent in 1927, a boarding school was established. A typical dormitory room for students is seen here in this 1930s photograph. The dormitory rooms were located on the third floor of the convent.

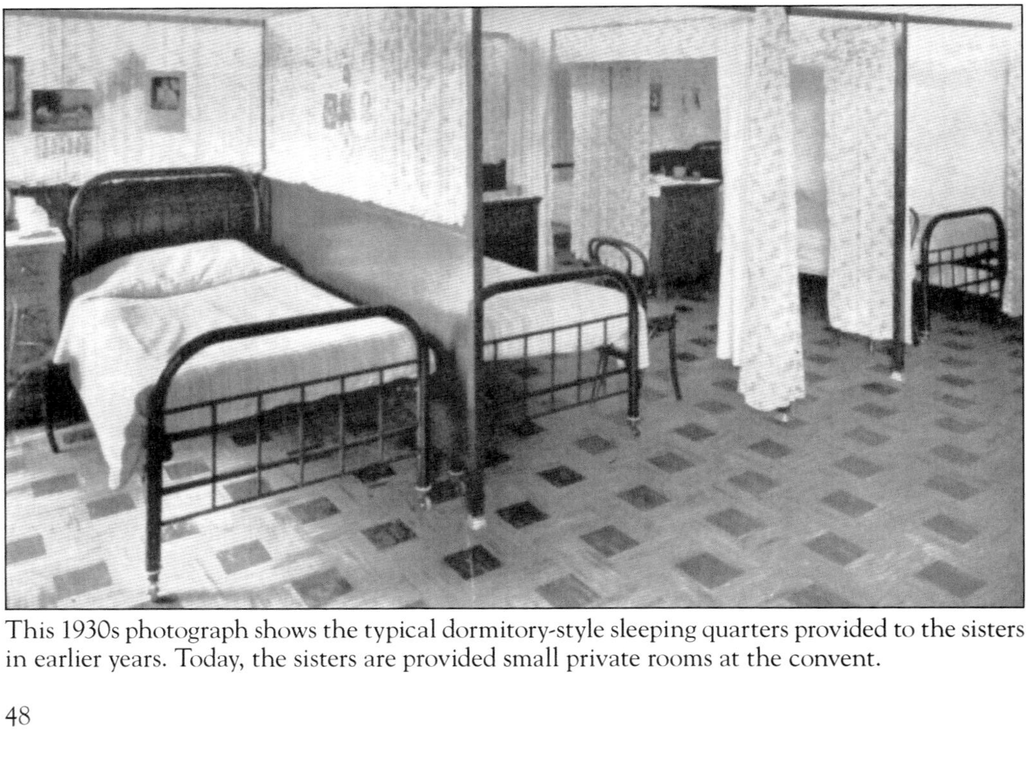

This 1930s photograph shows the typical dormitory-style sleeping quarters provided to the sisters in earlier years. Today, the sisters are provided small private rooms at the convent.

In 1960, two young twin sisters from Bellevue, Kentucky, entered the convent at St. Joseph Heights. Seen here praying in front of the Wayside Cross in 1961 are, from left to right, Sr. M. Charlynn and Sr. M. Shannon. The sisters are daughters of the Sacred Heart Parish.

This vintage photograph from the 1930s shows the subtle outline of sisters praying the Stations of the Cross. At the end of this pathway is the gateway to the Convent Cemetery.

St. Mary's Cemetery in Fort Mitchell is the final resting place for the Sisters of Notre Dame who died before 1922. The monument pictured is dedicated to the 67 sisters resting there in unmarked graves. (Courtesy of author.)

The open gateway to the Convent Cemetery welcomes all who visit the gravesite of the deceased members of the convent. Since 1924, three hundred sixteen sisters have found their final resting place in this small hilltop cemetery at St. Joseph Heights. (Courtesy of author.)

As seen in this 1958 photograph, two young novices pray by the gravesite of one of the departed sisters at the Convent Cemetery at St. Joseph Heights. As of March 31, 2011, three hundred ninety-two sisters from the Covington Province have gone to their eternal reward.

The statue of the Blessed Virgin welcomes residents to the east wing of the convent. This area contains the spiritual reading library, computer room, television room, and administrative offices. Lourdes Hall Care Center is located directly above the second floor and includes both medical care and assisted living facilities for the Sisters of the Covington Province. (Courtesy of author.)

Located on the third floor of the convent are a number of small, sparsely decorated guest rooms reserved for visitors to the Province House. As seen here, each room includes a single bed, night table, and desk with chair. (Courtesy of author.)

Four

Faces of the Covington Province

Four young aspirants enjoy themselves as they roller skate hand in hand around the convent grounds in this c. 1950 photograph. Pictured are, from left to right, Srs. M. Roselyn, Christine, Antony, and unidentified. The young lady on the far right decided to leave the convent after graduation from the academy.

In this 1928 photograph, two domestic workers pose outside the convent's kitchen delivery area, while the sister in charge observes from the kitchen entrance above. While domestic workers were used at times, it was the sisters themselves who were responsible for domestic services and food preparation. In recent years, a full-time lay kitchen staff has been employed to prepare three meals a day.

A number of sisters gathered in the convent's garden for this group portrait in 1930. Sr. M. Angela is seen seated in the center front. As provincial superior from 1924 to 1947, Sr. M. Angela served as the head of the Covington Province for the longest term in provincial history.

Postulants gather around the Christmas tree at St. Joseph Heights Convent in this 1952 photograph. In keeping with their vow of poverty, each sister was permitted to request three small gifts at Christmas. The gifts could include holy pictures, small religious articles, notebooks, or a dust cloth. Each sister and the superior would receive their requested gifts and a card with a poem inside from the Christ Child.

Sr. M. Constance (first row, far right) served as the director of aspirants for the Covington Province. She is pictured in front of the convent in 1932 with her group of young aspirants. Standing in the fourth row is Sr. M. Eleanor on the far left, and on the far right is Sr. Rita Marie (Casimira). Both of these sisters had distinguished careers as teachers at Villa Madonna College and Thomas More College. In the first row, second from left, is Sr. M. DeLellis, who dedicated the later part of her life to working with the children of Prince of Peace School in Covington.

The three traditional habits denoting the three stages in the process toward the professed life of a Sister of Notre Dame are shown in this photograph, taken around 1942. The young lady at left depicts the dress of the postulants, Sr. M. Carleta wears the habit of the novice on the right, and that of the professed sister is worn by Sr. M. Eleanor, shown at center. After Vatican II in 1962, modifications to the traditional habit began to take place.

Four sisters pose for this photograph on July 25, 1934, to commemorate their golden jubilee as Sisters of Notre Dame. Pictured are, from left to right, Srs. M. Emile, Caroline, Valena, and Cajetana. The photograph was taken on the rear lawn of the convent at St. Joseph Heights.

Sr. M. Angela sits peacefully reading her daily devotional. When Covington was designated as a province of the Sisters of Notre Dame in 1924, Sr. M. Angela was designated as the first provincial superior. She served as superior for more than 20 years and was instrumental in the growth and development of the Covington Province, including the construction of the convent at St. Joseph Heights. She had the unenviable task of guiding the province through the troubling years of World War II, the Depression, and the devastation of the 1937 flood.

Sr. M. Erma (left) and Sr. M. Ramilda (right) are seen here enjoying a friendly game of Scrabble after the day's work is done. Board games and card games of all kinds are a large part of the recreational activities enjoyed by the sisters.

Novices, postulants, and aspirants participate in a friendly game of volleyball at St. Joseph Heights Convent's multipurpose room. This room is located in the lower level of the convent and provided space for athletic activities, as well as events requiring a stage. The floor in this room was raised in the 1990s to provide access for the handicapped, thus enhancing its original purpose.

The love of crafts, such as ceramics and porcelain painting, has been a long-standing tradition with the Sisters of Notre Dame. Enjoying the evening's creative activity are, from left to right, Srs. M. Sheila, Bonaventure, Adelma, Christine, and Francello. The finished ceramic products were available for sale to support the convent or as gifts for family and benefactors who generously donated their services to the sisters.

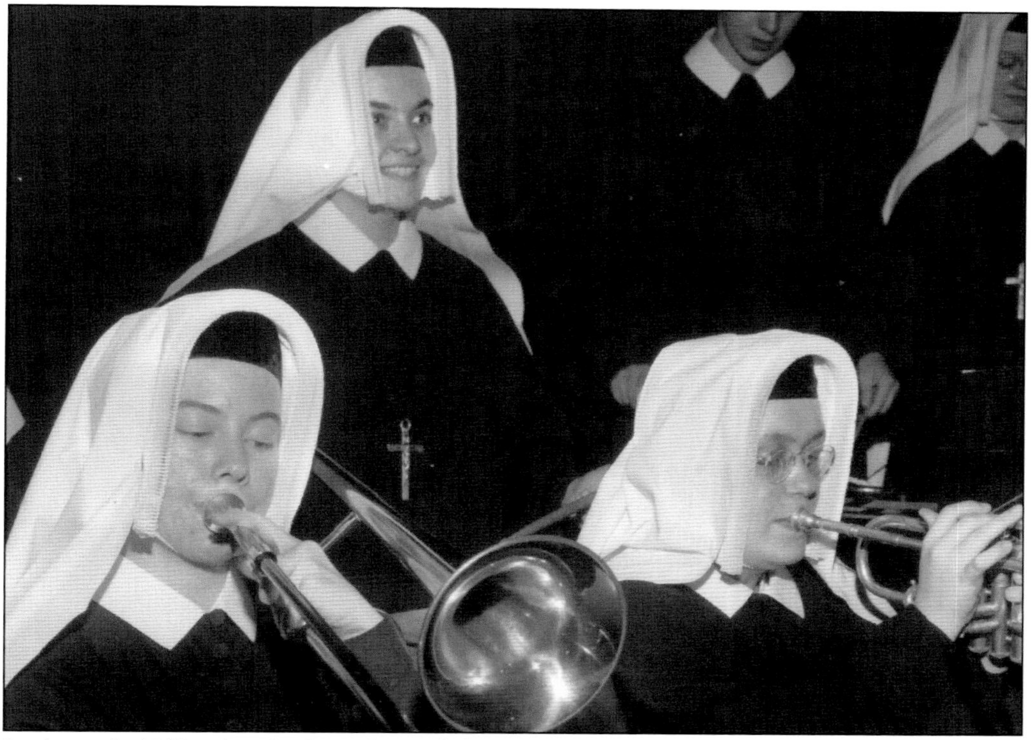

In the early 1960s, this rhythmic beat of the novices' pep band could be heard in the halls of the convent at St. Joseph Heights. Pictured are, from left to right, (first row) Sr. M. St. Josaph on the trombone and Sr. M. Edward (St. Eduard) on the trumpet; (second row) Sr. M. Shannon on the drums.

As they participate in the evening's recorder practice, the enjoyment of creating the sweet sound of music is evident on the faces of the young novices and postulants. This 1955 photograph was taken in the convent's music room, which doubled as the novices' study hall when band practice was finished.

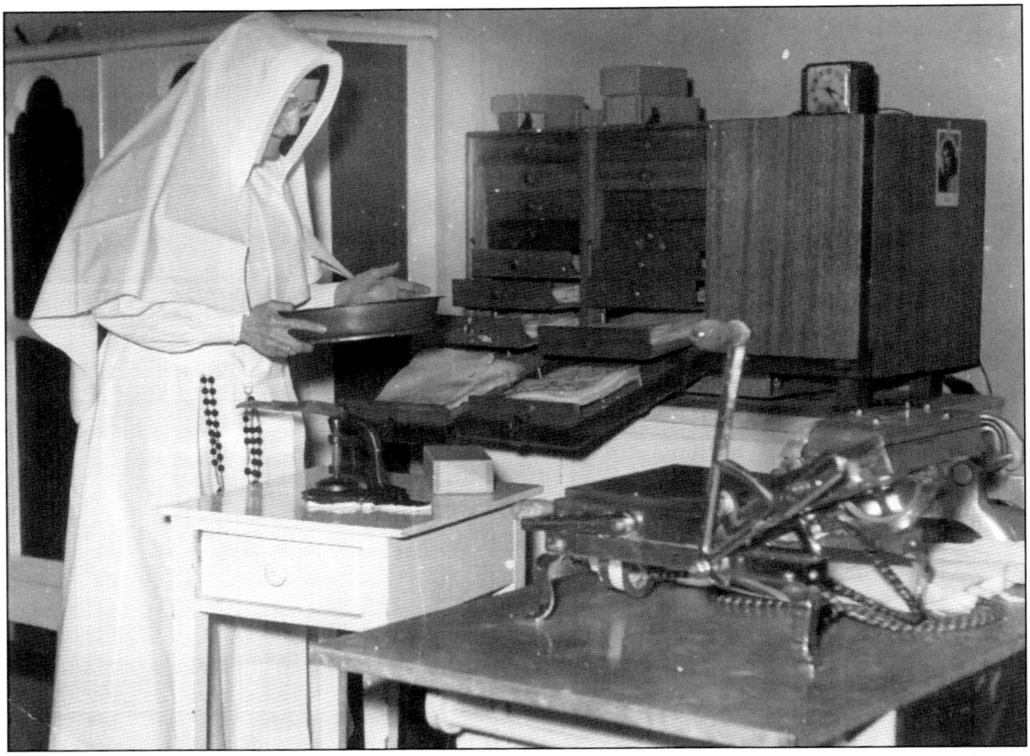

Sr. M. Corinne prepares the ingredients for host making. The Sisters of Notre Dame were responsible for making the hosts used throughout the Diocese of Covington in the celebration of the Mass. In the 1960s, the sisters relinquished the host-making business to the Passionist Sisters in Erlanger. Sr. M. Corinne was a daughter of the parish at St. John, Wilder.

Sr. M. Bathildis (left) and Sr. M. Laurene are seen operating the large mixer in the convent's kitchen at St. Joseph Heights. The two sisters worked together preparing daily meals at the convent from 1961 until 1993. Today, all kitchen duties are performed by a dedicated lay staff.

Each year, a day of appreciation was held at Marydale to thank the sisters of the diocese for their dedicated service in the parish schools. The religious of various orders in the diocese participated in the celebration of the Mass on the second floor of the barn and then were invited to enjoy a day of fun and food on the Marydale grounds. This photograph is from around 1960.

Mother M. Borromeo was the provincial superior of the Covington Province from 1959 until 1971. She is seen in this c. 1965 photograph on the grounds of the convent in the traditional habit of the Sisters of Notre Dame. It was during her term as provincial superior that Vatican II occurred, bringing forth many changes in religious life.

The wooden boat dock extending into the lake at Doctor Sperti's farm offered the ideal location for fishing for the big ones. The sisters, shown in this 1960 photograph, were stationed at the St. Aloysius Orphanage in Bond Hill, Ohio, and welcomed the day of fun and relaxation in the country.

Sister Marie (Edwarde) poses with the day's catch from the outing in 1960 at Doctor Sperti's Boone County farm.

The sisters from St. Aloysius Orphanage enjoyed the experience of touring Doctor Sperti's farm in this World War II Jeep. There is no indication why the decision was made to stop in the middle of the creek, but the image reflecting in the water provides a very interesting photograph from the 1960 picnic.

A summer picnic in the country in 1976 was the setting for Sr. M. Vincentia (left) to demonstrate her skill in riding a Yamaha motorcycle. Sr. M. Margene (right) helps create the illusion of wind in Sr. M. Vicentia's habit.

In this c. 1980 photograph, Sr. M. Eleanor (seated at left) and Sr. M. Joann (seated at right) review provincial documents, as Sr. M. Rose Paula looks on. Sr. M. Joann was the fifth provincial superior for the Covington Province from 1971 until 1983. Under her guidance, the construction of Joseph Hall was completed in 1980, adding a new east wing to the convent.

A procession of sisters return from the Convent Cemetery after the interment services for Sr. M. Agnetis in 1974. The chaplain of the Sisters at St. Joseph Heights, Fr. Allen Meier, conducted the graveside service. Sr. M. Agnetis is remembered fondly for her years of dedicated service as principal of old Notre Dame Academy in Covington and her legendary association with hotel magnate Conrad Hilton, which made the new Notre Dame Academy possible.

Sr. M. Paul Ann (left) and Sr. M. Laurence (right) were two of the committee members for the centennial celebration of the Sisters of Notre Dame's immigration to the United States and the introduction into the Covington Province in 1874. This 1974 photograph was taken at St. Agnes Church, Fort Wright.

In 1952, Sr. M. Vincentia (center) was called to Rome and asked to prepare a history of the congregation. After three years of research and writing, her book *Their Quiet Tread* was published in 1955. In this c. 1975 photograph, from left to right, Srs. Patricia Marie (Dianne Marie), Paula Marie, Vincentia, Michelyn, and Pamela Mae (Joan Marie) discuss the book.

Sr. Maria Therese has a bit of a problem with a broken string as she plays her favorite tune on her guitar. While she is an able guitarist, she is also an excellent teacher and administrator. Sister currently serves as principal at St. Augustine School in Covington.

Sr. M. Philomena plays a lively tune on her beloved violin from her bed in Lourdes Hall Care Center at St. Joseph Heights Convent around 1975. Sister was a very active member of the Covington Province and is especially remembered for her work on the July 4 picnic at the Heights. It was not unusual to find that Sister M. Philomena had negotiated for a new automobile; or in two instances, new homes to be used as major raffle prizes were arranged with her help.

Sr. M. Philip was a well respected history professor at Thomas More College. Sister also served as the archivist for the Provincial House, Thomas More College, and the Diocese of Covington. She was also fluent in several languages, which were quite helpful in translating historic documents and books for use in the archives.

The larger crucifix, on the left, is typical of those worn by the Sisters of Notre Dame with the vintage habit. In February 1976, the sisters began to wear the smaller crucifix on the right. The Sisters of the Covington Province gathered the larger crucifixes and had them melted down to make two silver cruets, two candlestick holders, and a silver cross for the convent's chapel. (Courtesy of author.)

Sr. M. Gregory Ann (standing) holds a ceramic wind chime that was made in her weekly class. As director, she provides instructions and technical assistance to the sisters who wish to participate in this creative activity. Seated are, from left to right, Srs. M. Ermelind, Lucilda (Prota), and Aquita. (Courtesy of the *Messenger*.)

Sisters of Notre Dame volunteers load trucks with needed supplies for the flood victims at Holy Trinity School in Harlan, Kentucky, in April 1977. St. Joseph Heights Convent served as a collection center for donated goods from Northern Kentucky and Cincinnati churches and organizations. The first two U-Haul trucks arrived at Holy Trinity School on April 12, some eight days after the flooding began. In all, the Sisters of Notre Dame were responsible for eight full truckloads of food, clothing, and personal care products arriving in Harlan to aid the victims of the flood.

On June 18, 1982, Mother Teresa, of Calcutta, arrived at St. Joseph Heights where she spent the night with the sisters at the convent. The next morning, after breakfast, she took a brief tour of the convent facilities and visited the sisters in Lourdes Hall Care Center. At that point, she was escorted by an official government automobile to Covington Catholic High School for a public outdoor prayer service and presentation officiated by Bishop Ackerman.

Four former provincial superiors of the Covington Province were together at the convent for this c. 1983 photograph. Those pictured are, from left to right, (seated) Sr. M. Borromeo (1959–1971) and Sr. M. Joseph (1947–1959); (standing) Sr. M. Joann (1971–1985) and Sr. M. Joell (1983–1986). In 1986, Sr. M. Joell was elected superior general of the Sisters of Notre Dame of Coesfeld.

In 1989, Superior General Sr. M. Joell visited the grave of Sr. M. Aloysia, foundress of the Sisters of Notre Dame. Sr. M. Aloysia passed away on May 6, 1889, and is buried in St. Joseph Cemetery in Cleveland, Ohio. The four candleholders in front of her headstone represent the four provinces in the United States: Cleveland, Toledo, Covington, and Thousand Oaks, California.

Sr. M. Shauna (provincial superior 1996–2005) receives a candle for the Covington Province from newly elected Superior General Sr. M. Sujita in Rome in 1998. Sr. M. Joell, the outgoing superior general, looks on as the presentation is made. (Courtesy of the *Messenger.*)

A fall afternoon visit to the Cincinnati Zoo provided a welcome break from the classroom. Those pictured are, from left to right, Srs. M. Joselle, Verda, and Paul Ann. This photograph was taken in 1985.

Sisters celebrate their silver jubilee in this 1983 photograph, taken at St. Joseph Heights Convent. Sisters pictured are, from left to right, Srs. Nancy Marie (Virginia Rose), M. Delrita, M. Joan Terese, M. Evelynn, and Mother Mary Joann.

On May 5, 1985, the sisters at St. Joseph Heights Convent celebrated Sr. M. Joell's (provincial superior) feast day with a program based on a Kentucky Derby theme. The sisters shown in the photograph each rode broomstick horses and raced around a designated track inside the convent's multipurpose room. The winner of the Notre Dame Academy Kentucky Derby was a horse by the name of "Sweet Blossom." Sr. M. Joell received a trophy and a corsage.

Sr. Maria Therese is seen taking her final vows in this 1988 photograph. Also, in attendance for the ceremony are, from left to right, Srs. Margaret Mary (Annette), Marla, and M. Margaret. Bishop William Hughes officiated at the service.

Sr. M. Joell served as provincial superior in the Covington Province for three years before being elected superior general of Sisters of Notre Dame of Coesfeld in 1986. Upon her relocation to the motherhouse in Rome, she was privileged to have an audience with Pope John Paul II at the Vatican. As seen in this 1986 photograph, Pope John Paul II presented Sr. M. Joell with a gift to commemorate the occasion.

Seven Sisters of Notre Dame pose in front of the convent at St. Joseph Heights for this group photograph of the staff at Notre Dame Academy. The sisters are, from left to right, (seated) Srs. M. Reina and Paul Ann; (standing) M. Judith (Lucienne), M. Dolores (Padraic), Marla, M. Rachel (Marlene), and M. Ethel (Lynne).

Sr. Marla is the current and ninth provincial superior of the Covington Province. Since taking office in 2005, she has guided the province through a period of growth and expansion, highlighted by the renovation of the Provincial House, the $12-million expansion program at Notre Dame Academy, and the establishment of the Notre Dame Urban Education Center in Covington.

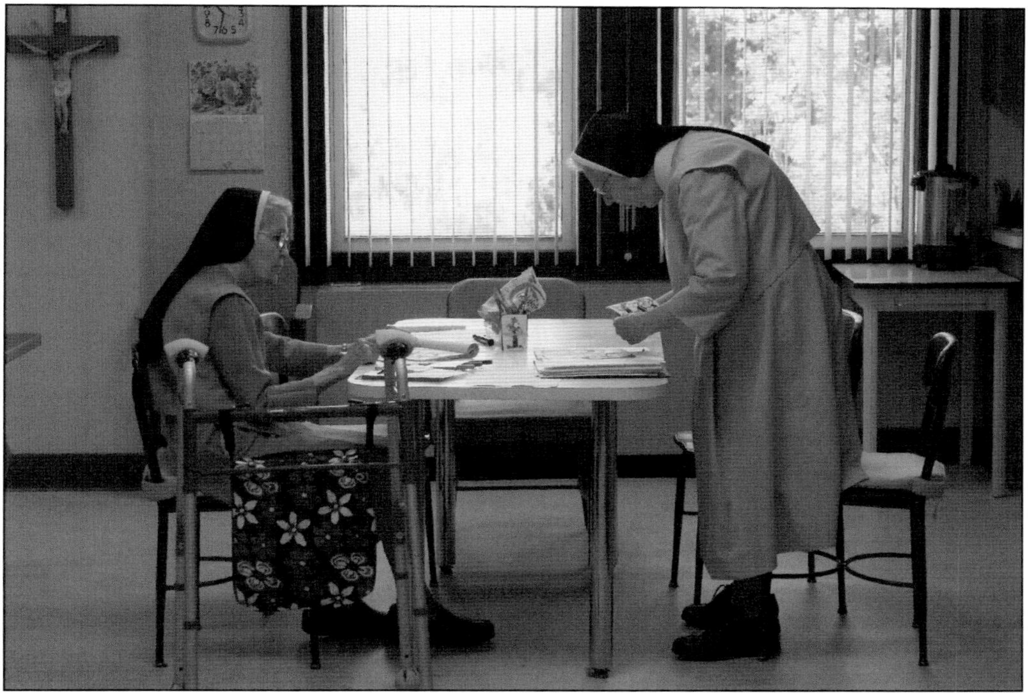

Each Thursday, a special activity program is prepared for the recreational enjoyment of the sisters at the convent. Sr. M. Francello (left) and Sr. M. Bernard Clare (right) are in charge of developing the theme and preparing the materials for this weekly gathering in room 234. (Courtesy of author.)

The main dining room at the convent is the hub of activity at mealtime each day. Here, four of the sisters take a break from their duties to enjoy lunch and conversation under the wall banner stating, "How Good God Is," which was St. Julie's favorite saying. The sisters pictured here are, from left to right, Srs. M. Francis, Dorothy Marie, M. Rosetta, and M. Magdelyn. (Courtesy of author.)

Sr. M. Joan Terese demonstrates the proper posture for riding the stationary bicycle. Besides enjoying frequent workout sessions in the convent's exercise room, Sr. M. Joan Terese is also busy with her work as archivist within the Provincial House at St. Joseph Heights. (Courtesy of author.)

Sr. M. Eloise celebrated her 100th birthday at a party with family and friends at St. Joseph Heights Convent in 2003. Sr. M. Eloise (1903–2006) was the longest living member of the Covington Province and served for 78 years. She is fondly remembered for her lively personality, sparkling eyes, and ever-present smile.

Five

School Days

While the Sisters of Notre Dame have provided a wide variety of services to the people of this region, they are most recognized for their work in educating the young. Through their dedicated efforts and spiritual guidance in the parish grade schools, high schools, and colleges, they have provided their students with a firm foundation on which to build a rewarding future. In this c. 1950 photograph, sister takes time out from the classroom to instruct her students on the fine art of the spiral pass. (Courtesy of St. John School.)

St. John Elementary School was one of the earliest affiliations established by the Sisters of Notre Dame. Three sisters were initially sent to St. John School in 1875. Sr. M. Vincentia had charge of the upper grades, Sr. M. Alfonsa taught the lower grades, and Sr. M. Coletta was in the kitchen. In 1910, the current site of the church and school, located on the Dixie Highway, was purchased for $10,300. (Courtesy of the *Messenger*.)

The seventh grade class from St. John School in Covington posed for this vintage photograph in 1937. One young lady, seen standing in the second row on the steps and to the far right, followed in the footsteps of her Notre Dame teachers by joining the convent after graduation. The future Sr. M. Kathlyn, along with three of her siblings—Srs. M. Ann Adele, Stefanie, and Ann Therese—would all become Sisters of Notre Dame. (Courtesy of St. John School.)

Sr. M. DeLellis offers a pleasant smile as she sits with her beloved piggy bank, which she used to solicit contributions to support various programs at Prince of Peace School (formerly St. John School) in Covington. In 1986, the school was renamed and currently serves students from the parishes of St. John, Mother of God, St. Ann, and Sts. Boniface and James. (Courtesy of the *Messenger.*)

Spirits were high at Prince of Peace School, as the Cincinnati Bengals prepared for their Super Bowl XXIII appearance in 1989. Sr. M. Brenden welcomed the opportunity to lead her students in a rousing cheer of support for the team. (Courtesy of St. John School.)

St. Augustine School in Covington is another of the earliest affiliations for the Sisters of Notre Dame. The sisters have served the families of the parish since 1875 and continue to teach in the school today. Records indicate that Sr. M. Cecilia, the future superior general of the entire congregation, taught music and choir at St. Augustine School in 1876–1877.

Sr. M. Karlanne and a group of students from St. Augustine School in Covington enjoy a casual study session in this 1980 photograph. In the early years, St. Augustine School experienced rapid growth, and by 1918, the enrollment had reached 316 students.

First grade students were dressed in their finest clothes for this 1887 class photograph at St. Stephen School in Newport, Kentucky. The affiliation with St. Stephen Parish was established in 1875 and continues to this day with two sisters living at the St. Stephen Parish Convent next to the church.

This photograph from the early 1890s shows the first grade students at St. Stephen School. The large number of students in the class was fairly typical for the urban schools of the time period.

The Sisters of Notre Dame arrived at St. John the Baptist School in Wilder, Kentucky, in 1909. The sisters served in the parish and operated the school until 1981. While the school has closed its doors after 134 years of educating children, St. John the Baptist Parish continues to thrive today with over 100 registered families. The present stone church was constructed in 1858.

An all-school photograph of the students and their two Sisters of Notre Dame teachers was taken outside the school in 1933. The sisters pictured are, from left to right, Sr. M. Sophia and Sr. M. Clementy. St. John the Baptist Church and School have served the parish and community since prior to the Civil War.

Sr. Eleanor Marie (Celsa) works with a young girl at the sewing machine, as Srs. M. Rosarina (center) and Sophia (right) assist with the fabric selection in this c. 1950 photograph. The young ladies were members of the 4-H Club at St. John the Baptist School.

The Sisters of Notre Dame have had an 88-year affiliation with St. Martin of Tours School in Cheviot, Ohio. Beginning in 1912, one year after the parish was established, until the year 2000, the sisters taught in the school and served the parish. St. Martin of Tours Parish observed its centennial celebration in 2010–2011.

Sr. M. Domitilla poses with her 1934 class from St. Agnes in Bond Hill, Ohio. Also seen in this photograph is Henrietta Lamping, located in the third row, second from the right, who eventually joined the Sisters of Notre Dame and took the name Sr. M. Thaddeus. The affiliation with St. Agnes School existed from 1893 to 1981.

The schoolchildren of St. John in Carrollton, Kentucky, stand in front of the church and school in this 1853 photograph. The Sisters of Notre Dame taught in the school from 1875 until 1972. The sisters also taught religion classes from 1978 until 1983.

Classes for the children of St. William Parish in Lancaster, Kentucky, were held in this renovated two-story residence. Prior to the renovation, the residence included the normal family living spaces and also slave quarters within the main building. The Sisters of Notre Dame taught at St. William School from 1952 until 1965. This photograph is from 1952.

In the early 1950s, the sisters from St. William School in Lancaster, Kentucky, would travel to Mount Vernon, Kentucky, to provide religious instruction to the area children. Here, Sr. M. Josine conducts religion class in the back room of Reynold's General Store in this c. 1952 photograph.

The Sisters of Notre Dame have been affiliated with St. Augustine School in Augusta, Kentucky, since 1875 until the present. Sr. M. Eduard (St. Eduard) and Fr. Louis Brinker pose with the children in this 1968 First Communion photograph.

Sr. M. Margaret discusses a photograph with some of the students at St. Therese School in Southgate, Kentucky. The display was part of the Catholic School Week Celebration in 1976. The Sisters of Notre Dame taught at St. Therese from 1968 until 2008.

The Sisters of Notre Dame have been affiliated with St. Agnes Parish and School in Fort Wright, Kentucky, since its beginning in 1930. Prior to St. Agnes constructing their own school in 1941, the students from the parish were sent to the school run by the sisters at St. Joseph Heights. This 1940 photograph shows the combined classes with their teacher Sr. M. Terentia.

Srs. M. Clareta (left) and Edwardine (right) direct their students as they rehearse for a school program in the c. 1970 photograph. The Sisters of Notre Dame were affiliated with St. Agnes School from 1930 until 1995. During that time frame, St. Agnes School grew to one of largest in the Diocese of Covington. After a gap of 12 years, a sister from Notre Dame rejoined the staff of St. Agnes School in 2007.

The school day is over, and the students at St. Agnes wait to board the buses for home in this c. 1955 photograph. In late August 1930, the diocese notified the Sisters of Notre Dame that a new school would be opened on Old State Road in Fort Wright and the sisters would be in charge. Srs. M. Idlephons and Angeleen were given the task of opening the school in the old Knochelman residence within a few weeks. On September 8, the school was opened with an enrollment of 32 students.

In this c. 1974 photograph, Sisters of Notre Dame are seen exiting St. Charles Church in Carthage, Ohio. The Sisters of Notre Dame were affiliated with the parish school from 1924 until 1992. The two sisters exiting the church arm in arm are, from left to right, Srs. M. Evangela and M. Cecile (Cecil).

The Sisters of Notre Dame taught in St. Mark School, Richmond, Kentucky, from 1966 to 1993. Posing next to the school are, from left to right, Srs. Joanne Marie (Agnes Marie), Ann Marie (Dortheea), Elaine Marie (Doramarie), and M. Joanne (Edward Anne) in the white habit.

Sisters of Notre Dame attended Mass celebrating the centennial anniversary of the sisters' presence at St. Mary's Parish in Alexandria, Kentucky, in this 1976 photograph. The sisters' affiliation with St. Mary School began in 1876. In 1950, St. Mary High School was established, and in 1961, the name was changed to Bishop Brossart High School.

St. Joseph Parish and School in Cold Spring, Kentucky, are closely linked with St. Joseph Diocesan Orphanage. The Sisters of Notre Dame served St. Joseph School until 2008 and resided at the first parish convent depicted in this c. 1964 photograph.

In 1946, the Sisters of Notre Dame began teaching and working with the Native American residents at St. Augustine Mission in Winnebago, Nebraska. Sr. M. Miriam is seen with students in this c. 1950 photograph. This affiliation with the mission concluded in 1954.

The beginning of the school library is seen in this c. 1950 photograph, taken at Sacred Heart School in Bellevue, Kentucky. The Sisters of Notre Dame began teaching at the school in 1876, just two years after the parish was established. In 1987, the name of the school was changed to St. Michael, and then in 2002, the name of school was changed to Holy Trinity.

In 1937, the Sisters of Notre Dame sent members of the Covington Province to work with the children at the Immaculata Mission in Birmingham, Alabama. The sisters taught in the high school until 1966 but continued their work at Our Lady of Fatima Elementary School until 2001. Sr. M. Leonette is seen in this c. 1970 photograph with four altar boys she trained at the mission school.

Kindergarten class at St. Joseph Heights provided an exciting time for both students and teachers in the 1950s. Sr. M. Patricia (Michele) (left) and Sr. M. Alonsa (right) enjoyed the daily interaction with the children attending the kindergarten classes, which were offered from 1949 to 1958.

Due to the use of inappropriate eyedrops while infants were still in the hospital, a large number of area children lost their eyesight. In 1957, the Sisters of Notre Dame began operating a school for the children who were blind at Mother of God School. In 1962, the school was relocated to Sacred Heart School in Bellevue. The School for the Blind was closed in 1968 because of a significant reduction in the number of children who had lost their sight. Srs. M. Leopolda and Roselyn were the initial instructors, with Srs. M. Bernard Clare and Francello taking charge in 1958.

Sr. M. Margaret (left) and Sr. M. Paulla (right) enjoy a discussion about the mission display at St. Columban School in Loveland, Ohio. The Sisters of Notre Dame were first introduced into the school in 1926 and continue their dedicated service to St. Columban Parish and School today.

Shown in this c. 1860 photograph is the first school building of St. Peter and Paul Parish in California, Kentucky. The first school opened in 1858 and was staffed by lay teachers. The Sisters of Notre Dame entered the school in 1956 and continued their work in the parish until 1972.

The Sisters of Notre Dame taught at Holy Trinity School from 1957 until 2006. Seen in this 1970 photograph are five of the sisters who were assigned to the Harlan, Kentucky, school at that time. They are, from left to right, Srs. Marianna (Herman Joseph), Marjorie Marie (Joseph Anne), M. Jerome, M. Barbara Jean, and M. Virganne.

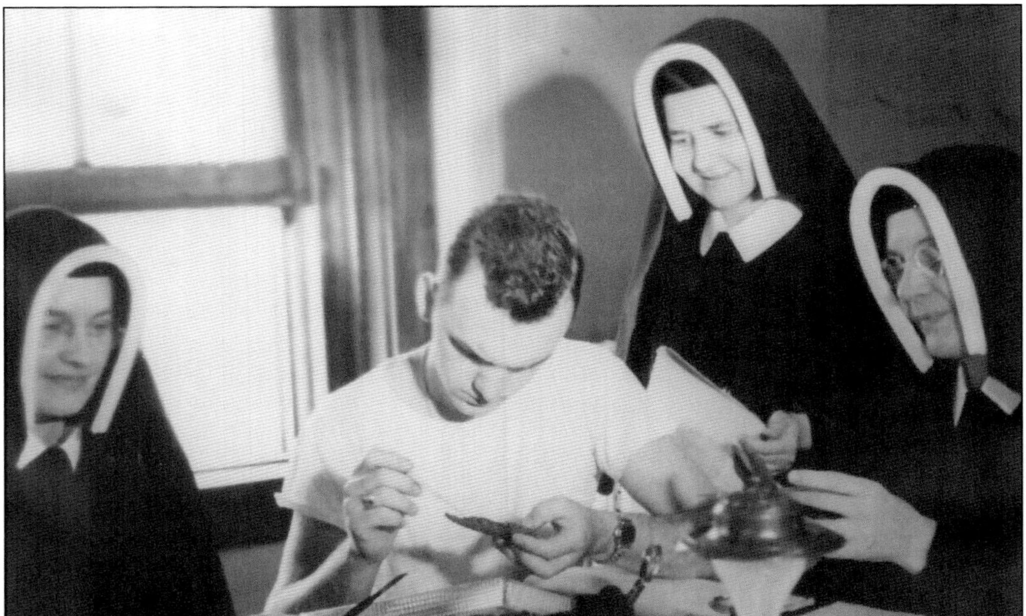

Three Sisters of Notre Dame assist a student with his science project at Villa Madonna College in Covington in this c. 1950 photograph. The sisters are, from left to right, Srs. M. Ancille, Noelita, and Paul. The Sisters of Notre Dame have been members of the staff since 1928.

Sr. M. Carlotta is seen in this c. 1952 photograph instructing her students at Villa Madonna College in Covington, Kentucky. Seated in the traditional habit is Sr. M. Margaret Agnes. The Sisters of Notre Dame have been affiliated with the college since 1928. The college is currently known as Thomas More College.

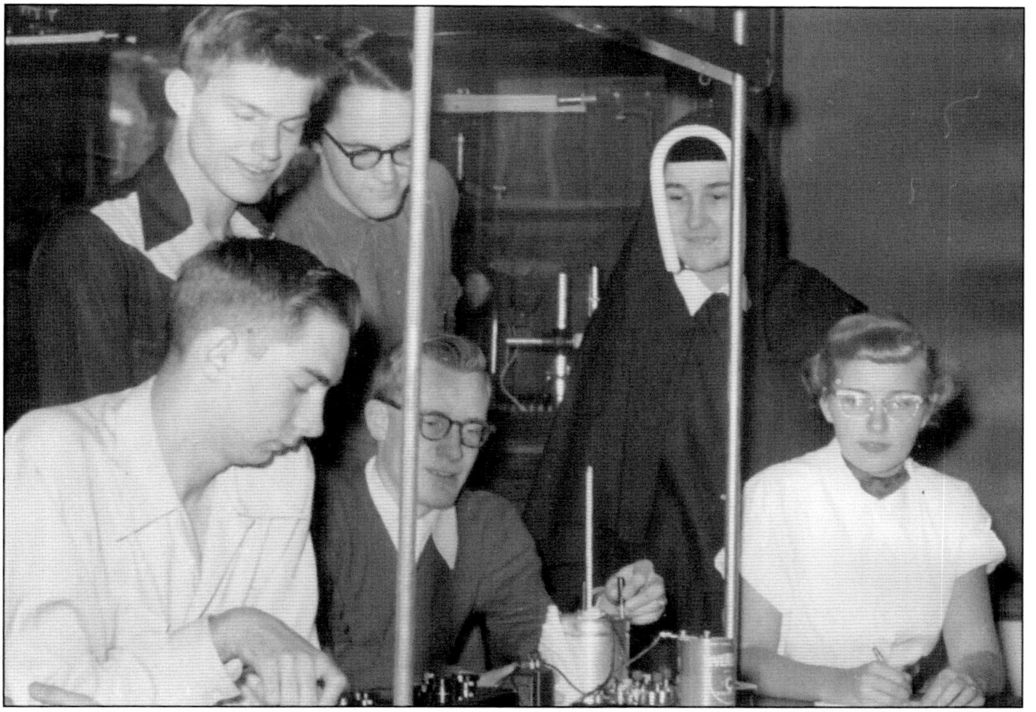

Sr. M. Eleanor observes the students in her class, as they conduct a physics experiment at Villa Madonna College in the 1950s. Villa Madonna College was established in 1923 as a college to educate young women as teachers. In 1945, the college was designated coeducational. In 1968, the college was relocated to a new campus in Crestview Hills. The name was also changed to Thomas More College at that time.

In 1949, St. Mary Parish in Alexandria, Kentucky, purchased the former Campbell County High School building, which is shown in the photograph. The building became the home for the parish elementary and high schools (now Bishop Brossart High School). (Courtesy of Bishop Brossart High School.)

Sr. M. Cyril is shown in the c. 1965 photograph tutoring one of the students at Bishop Brossart High School. The Sisters of Notre Dame began their affiliation with St. Mary Parish and schools in 1876 and have taught at both the elementary and secondary levels. (Courtesy of Bishop Brossart High School.)

Students in Sr. M. Julitta's class (1964–1965) at Bishop Brossart High School turn to face the camera for this classroom photograph around 1964. In 1962, the former St. Mary High School was renamed in honor of Bishop Ferdinand Brossart, the fourth bishop of the Covington Diocese. (Courtesy of Bishop Brossart High School.)

Sr. M. Tereze discusses a class assignment with one of her students at Bishop Brossart High School. At this time, Sr. M. Tereze is the only Sister of Notre Dame assigned to the high school, where she has served as an instructor or director of student affairs and guidance since 1977.

The statue of Our Lady of Grace stands with open arms to welcome all who come to Notre Dame Academy. Two families whose girls were graduates from the academy in years past donated the white marble statue to the school. With its foundation dating back over 100 years, Notre Dame Academy continues to educate young women and prepare them to make a difference in their community and the world. (Courtesy of author.)

While there have been many who have contributed to the growth and success of Notre Dame Academy, Sr. M. Agnetis is certainly the most legendary. While principal of the academy from 1920 until 1946, Sr. M. Agnetis may be most remembered for her providential relationship with hotel magnate Conrad Hilton, which ultimately made the dream of the new Notre Dame Academy a reality.

While on a business trip to Cincinnati, Conrad Hilton visited St. Joseph Heights and toured the alfalfa field, which would eventually become the site for the new Notre Dame Academy. The May 21, 1956, visit included, from left to right, Alvin and Mary Aldemeyer, Conrad Hilton, and Olive Wakemen, Hilton's secretary. This was the only occasion that Hilton visited the site. He and Sr. M. Agnetis continued to correspond until her death in 1974.

From left to right, Sr. M. Emmanuel (the local superior and coordinator) and Sr. M. Immacula (the principal) review the architectural drawings for the new Notre Dame Academy in this c. 1962 photograph. The new facility was designed for 600 students, with a residence for 35 sisters, at a cost of approximately $2 million.

After a six-year fundraising effort by the Sisters of Notre Dame, donations made by the local communities, and a $500,000 pledge by Conrad Hilton, ground was broken for the new Notre Dame Academy on April 16, 1961. The new $2-million academy was formally dedicated on March 1, 1964, the ninth anniversary of Sr. M. Agnetis's first letter to Mr. Hilton.

Notre Dame Academy has continued to grow since the academy was relocated to its current home at St. Joseph Heights. The programs and facilities are constantly being evaluated, and numerous modifications have been made over the last 45 years. The most recent is the $12-million Performing Arts Center and facilities expansion. Viewing the site from atop the construction equipment are, from left to right, Srs. M. Ethel (Lynne), Shauna, and Rachel (Marlene) and on ground level are Srs. M. Paul Ann, Dolores (Padraic), and Lea (Berndette).

From left to right, Sr. Elaine Marie (Doramarie, former principal) and Sr. M. Shauna (former president) wear their construction hard hats as they make an inspection tour of the new Performing Arts Center addition in 2008. Both were members of the building committee and were instrumental in creating a facility in which Notre Dame Academy can move into the 21st century.

The present-day Notre Dame Academy is dedicated in this 2010 photograph. Since 1906, tens of thousands of young women have had the advantage of being educated by the Sisters of Notre Dame. Today's academy is well prepared to meet the educational challenges of the future and to welcome the young women of the next generation. (Courtesy of author.)

Six

Service beyond the Classroom

Irene Nichols, a veteran teacher of the primary grades at St. Thomas School in Fort Thomas, Kentucky, created this 20-inch-tall, handcrafted doll with a vintage habit. The doll accurately depicts the original habit worn by the Sisters of Notre Dame of Coesfeld, Germany, in 1850. The doll has been publicly displayed at the convent and is currently housed in the archives at the Provincial House. (Courtesy of author.)

St. Joseph Diocesan Orphanage was established by Bishop August Toebbe in 1870. Originally a home for orphaned boys, the facility was located on what was known as the Walsh Farm on US 27 in Cold Spring, Kentucky, until 1961. The site is presently the home of the Disabled American Veterans (DAV), Northern Kentucky Headquarters.

The Sisters of Notre Dame accepted full charge of St. Joseph Diocesan Orphanage in 1877 and operated the home continuously until its closing in 1961. Young residents enjoyed themselves on the orphanage's playground in this c. 1930 photograph.

On several occasions, young girls were relocated from other Catholic orphanages to St. Joseph for temporary housing. In 1885, the diocese decided that both boys and girls should be permanent residents, thus avoiding the separation of brothers and sisters within a family. This c. 1940 photograph shows the young girls of St. Joseph Diocesan Orphanage on the steps of the facility, near the playground.

The sisters made sure that the children had nutritious meals and proper table manners, as seen in this photograph from around 1950. The first meal provided to the original group of children in 1877 was the result of going door-to-door and begging neighbors for food.

Sr. M. Alice (John Carl) plays the piano, as the young girls at St. Joseph Diocesan Orphanage play a game of "musical rug." This photograph was taken around 1950.

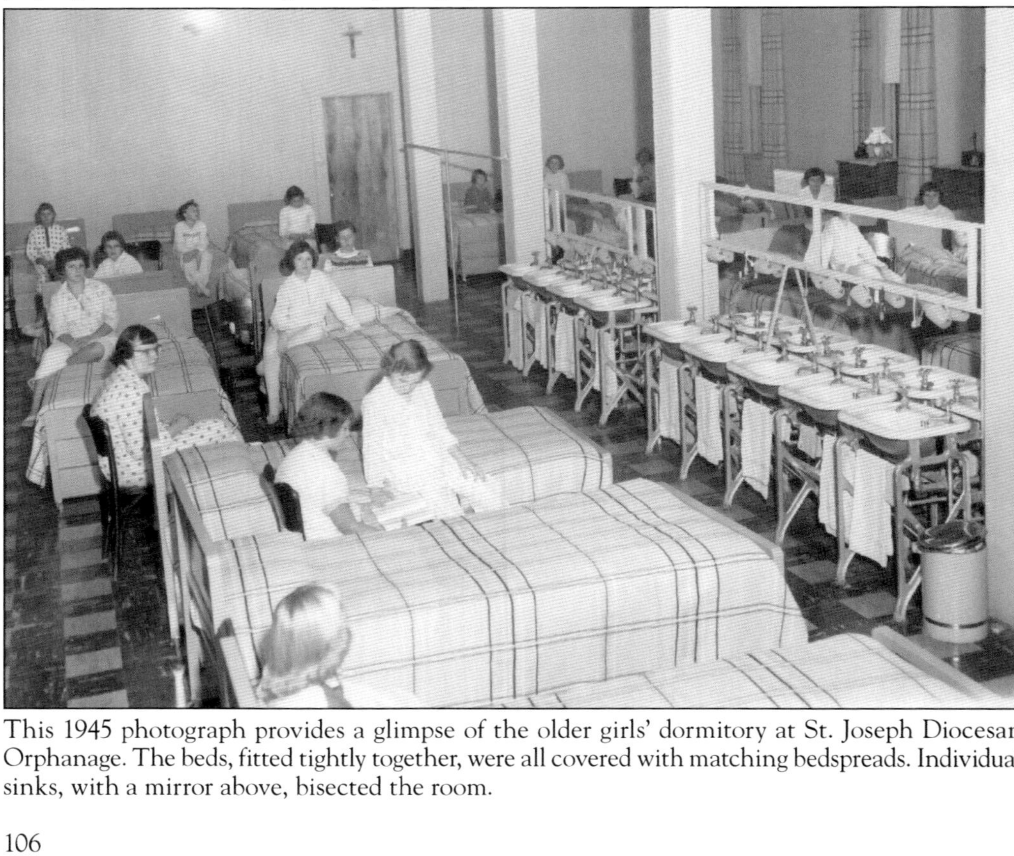

This 1945 photograph provides a glimpse of the older girls' dormitory at St. Joseph Diocesan Orphanage. The beds, fitted tightly together, were all covered with matching bedspreads. Individual sinks, with a mirror above, bisected the room.

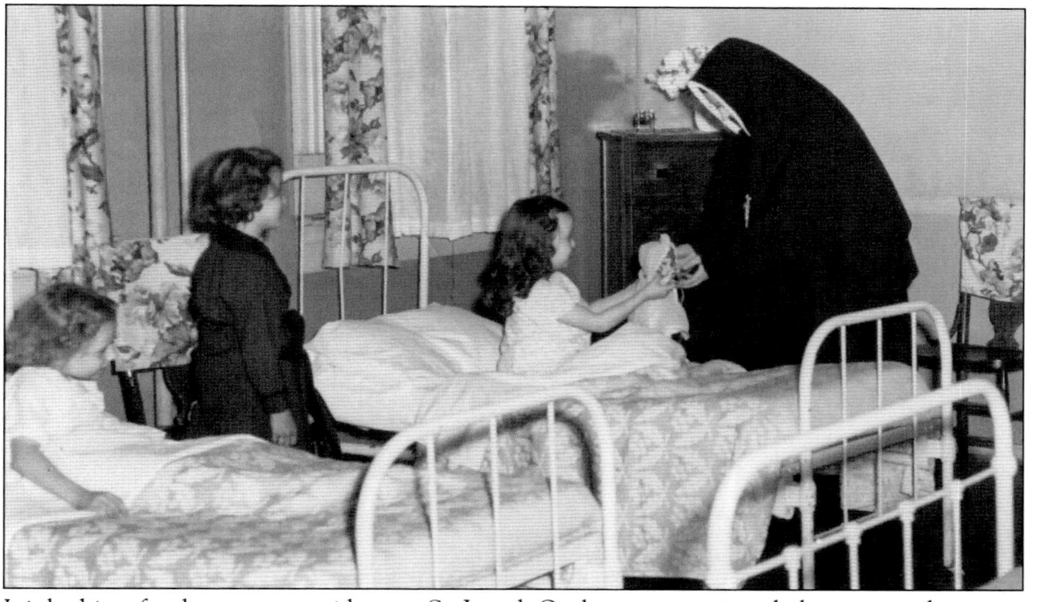

It is bedtime for the younger residents at St. Joseph Orphanage, as a sister helps prepare the young girl and her doll for a good night's sleep. This photograph was taken around 1945.

Preschool children at St. Joseph Diocesan Orphanage sit patiently awaiting their holiday treats during the Christmas season in 1951. The younger children were kept at the home for kindergarten and elementary school. Older children were relocated to foster homes in order to attend local high schools.

With the sister in white supervising, the older girls do the yearly chore of canning at the orphanage in this 1944 photograph. Fruits and vegetables grown on the grounds of the orphanage were an important part of the diet of both the children and staff.

Sr. M. Perpetua, in the white habit, works with some of the older girls in the kitchen at St. Joseph Diocesan Orphanage in this 1944 photograph. Learning the fine points of meal preparation was not only helpful at the orphanage but also beneficial to the young ladies in their future lives.

Laundry day at St. Joseph Diocesan Orphanage provided the young residents with the opportunity to work as a team, and at the same time to receive individual instructions from the sisters on ironing and folding. This photograph was taken around 1945.

On any given day at the orphanage, one could find the young boys enjoying themselves in a pick-up game of baseball or basketball. On this afternoon in 1945, one of the young gentlemen finds a unique way to view his world, as the camera records the moment.

Sr. M. Celine (far right) and two other sisters monitor the junior boys on the playground, as the older boys, in the rear, return from a game of baseball. As indicated by this 1955 photograph, Roy Rogers and Gene Autry were the big heroes of the day.

The Sisters of Notre Dame commemorated 75 years of service at St. Joseph Diocesan Orphanage with dinner and celebration at the orphanage in 1952. Approximately 60 sisters who had served at the orphanage were in attendance.

St. Aloysius Orphanage on Reading Road in the Bond Hill section of Cincinnati, Ohio, is another of the earliest affiliations for the Sisters of Notre Dame. The sisters served at St. Aloysius from 1877 until 2000.

Nineteen of the Sisters of Notre Dame who resided at St. Aloysius Orphanage are seen in this 1943 photograph. The young priest in the center is Fr. Francis Lay, a former resident at the home. To the left of Father Lay is Sr. M. Edwardine who served at the home for a total of 18 years, beginning 1929 until the late 1940s.

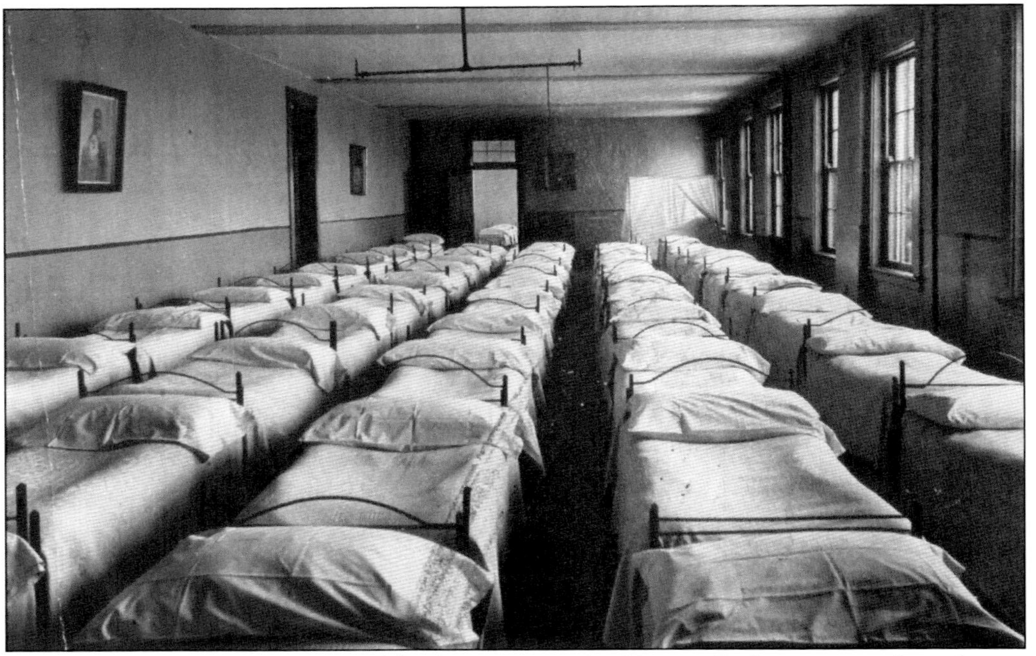

This very early photograph of one of the dormitories at St. Aloysius Orphanage provides a glimpse of the overcrowded, but neatly kept, living circumstance existing in the late 19th century.

This 1944 photograph shows some of the younger children in their classroom at St. Aloysius Orphanage. While the sisters' service at St. Aloysius was spiritually rewarding, earthly compensation was meager at best. Each sister was paid a grand sum of $50 per year in 1877, with payments of $4.17 being made monthly.

Sr. M. Francello entertains two preschool children by reading them a storybook. The bookshelf behind is lined with childhood favorites such as *Little Stories for Little People*, *Barnyard Babies*, *Five Little Pussy Cats*, and *Bobby Bear.* The c. 1951 photograph was taken at St. Aloysius Orphanage.

Sr. M. Rosetta, the group mother, sends two of her young charges off to a day at school in 1962. In 1961, St. John's and St. Joseph's Children's Homes merged to form the Diocesan Catholic Children's Home (DCCH) in Fort Mitchell, Kentucky.

Sr. M. Michyl, the group mother at Diocesan Catholic Children's Home, serves the children an after-school snack in the c. 1978 photograph. The Sisters of Notre Dame have served there since 1957 and continue today.

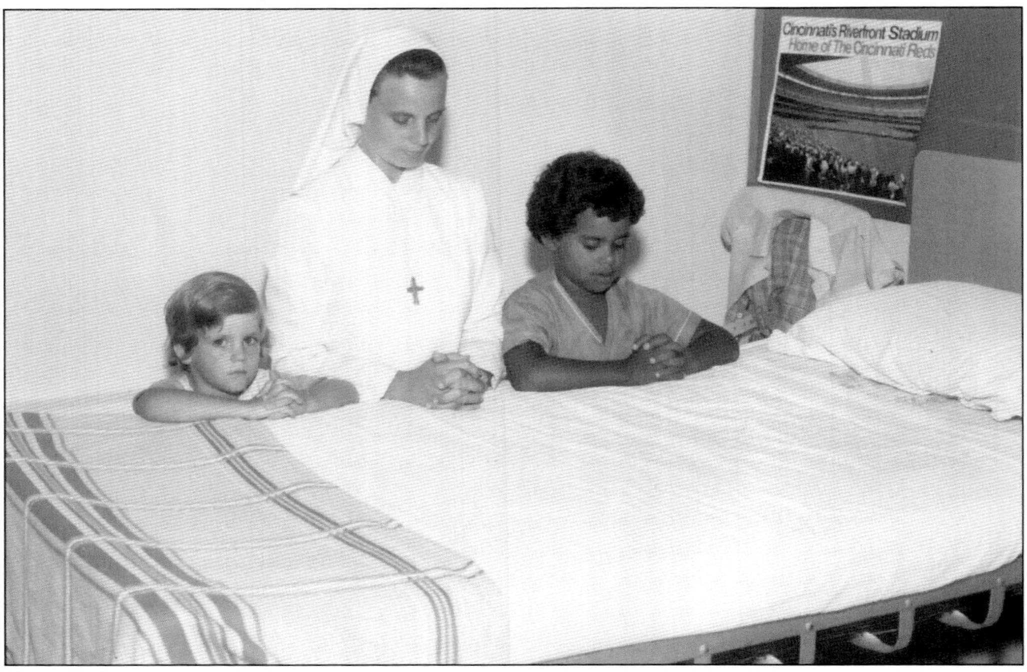

Sr. Jean Marie joins two young residents seen reciting their nightly prayers in this 1976 photograph. Sr. Jean Marie has served at the Diocesan Catholic Children's Home for the past 37 years, and since 1989, she has held the position of executive director.

Sr. M. Martine is seen working at her sewing machine in this c. 1935 photograph. Beginning in 1934, the Sisters of the Covington Province provided domestic service as a means of generating income to help reduce the debt on the convent at St. Joseph Heights. The domestic service was provided outside the convent at various locations, such as the Paulist Generalate in New York and the Viatorian Seminary in Washington, DC.

St. Charles Care Center in Covington, Kentucky, is the Covington Province's only adult care facility. The Sisters of Notre Dame have been affiliated with St. Charles since 1961. A menu of services from independent living, assisted living, and skilled nursing care is available on the campus.

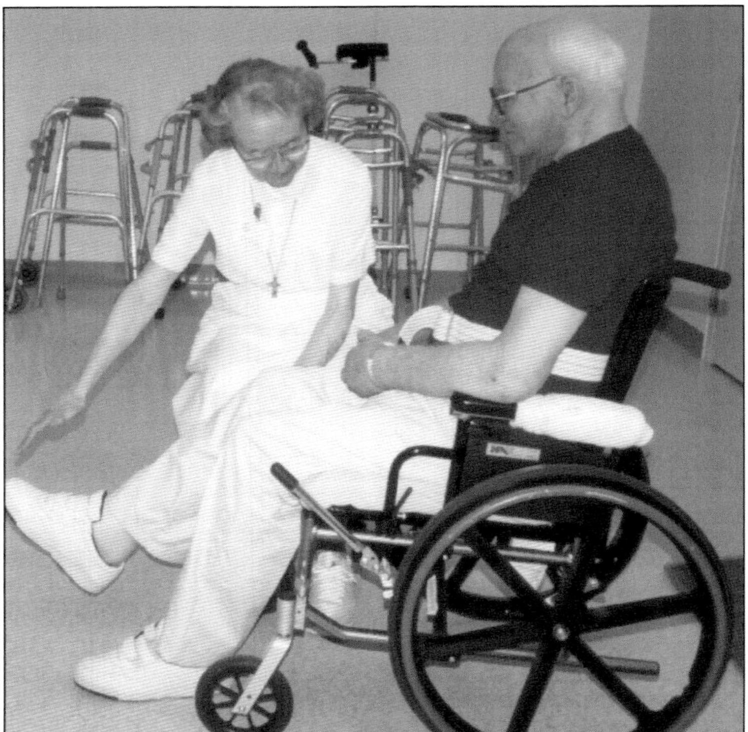

The 11 sisters from the Covington Province, shown in this photograph, are the original members of the nursing staff sent to St. Charles Care Center in 1961. Sr. M. Edwin, seated in the first row center, was the first administrator at St. Charles.

Physical therapist Sr. M. Jean Clare works with one of her resident patients at St. Charles Care Center. A wide range of therapeutic services are provided on site by an outside group of professional therapists.

Sr. M. Amatis assists one of the residents with her meal at St. Charles Care Center. Sr. M Amatis was in charge of the kitchen and was the dietary supervisor at the center. Sister entered the Sisters of Notre Dame in Mulhausen, Germany, in 1931 and came to America as a novice.

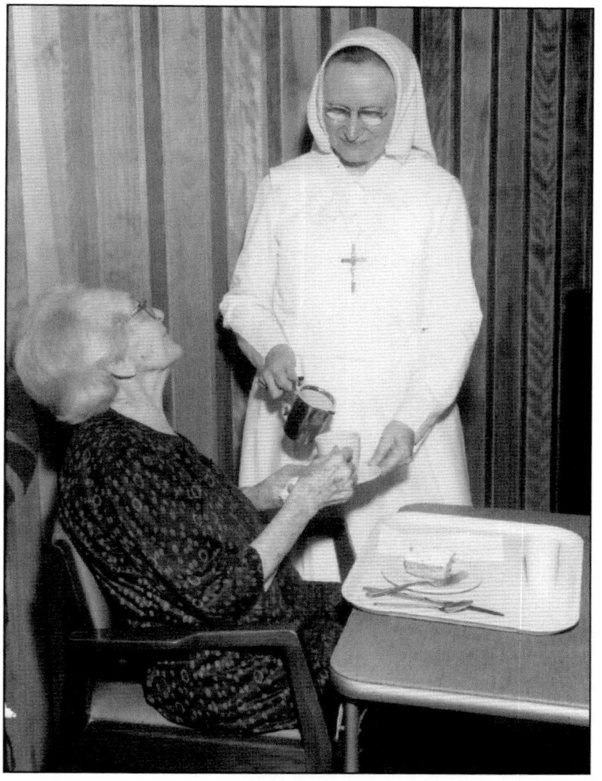

Sisters, in their white habits, take a few minutes to gather together to celebrate the Christmas season at St. Charles Care Center in 1964.

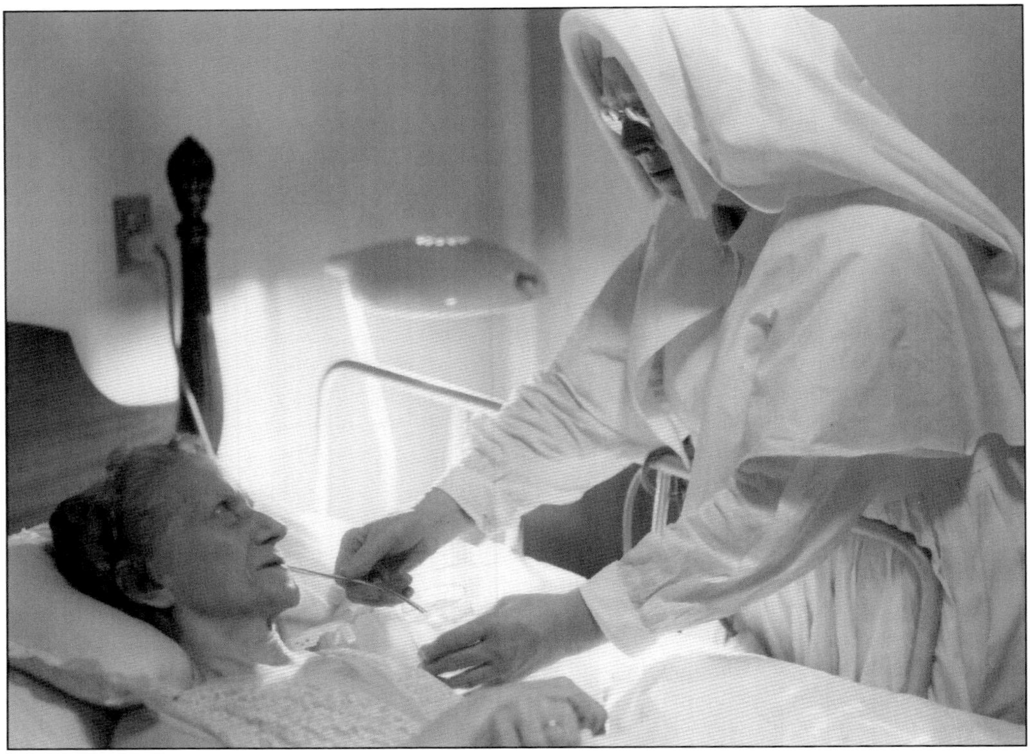

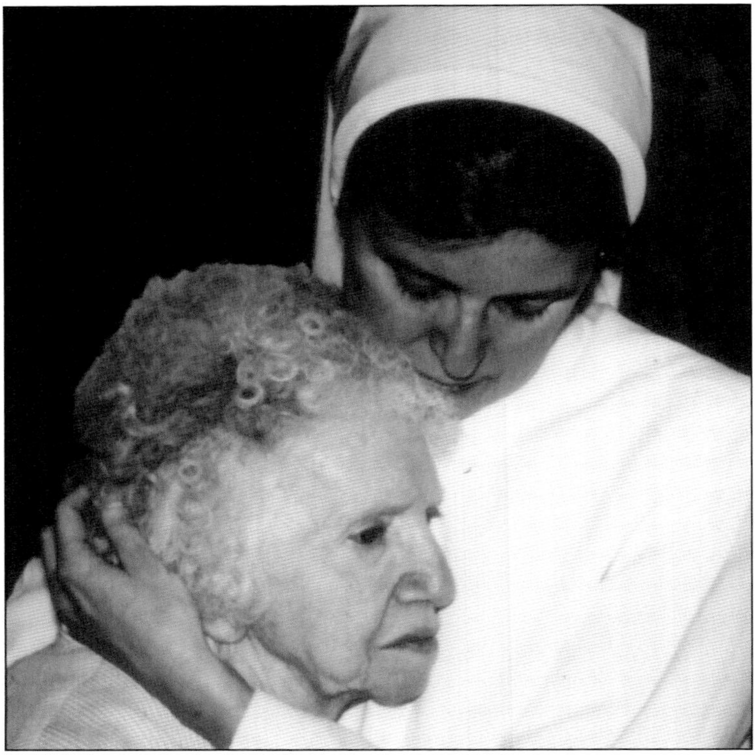

Sr. M. Briget helps a patient take a sip of water at St. Charles Care Center in this c. 1970 photograph. Sr. M. Briget served at the center for 17 years, from 1961 until 1978.

Sr. M. Luann comforts one of her patients at St. Charles Care Center. Sr. M. Luann is the current administrator at the St. Charles Care Center where she has served since 1977.

The Notre Dame Hospital in Lynch, Kentucky, was owned and operated by the Sisters of Notre Dame from 1951 until 1961. The hospital was previously owned by the United States Coal and Coke Company and was constructed in 1920 to serve the medical needs of Appalachian coal miners and their families. (Courtesy of the Diocese of Covington.)

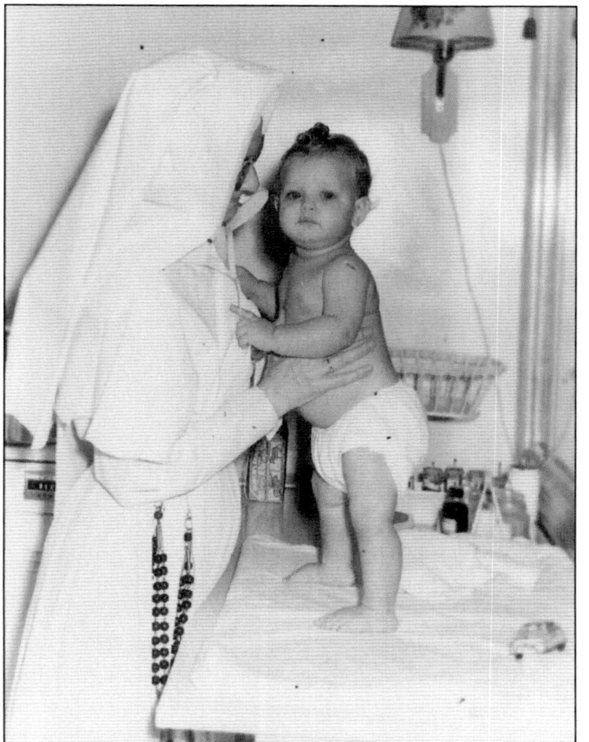

A young child is comforted by Sr. M. Rosilda at Notre Dame Hospital in this c. 1955 photograph. The hospital and all of the equipment was sold to the Sisters of Notre Dame for $1 in 1950. Notre Dame Hospital became the first hospital owned by the Sisters of Notre Dame of the Covington Province in the United States.

The Sisters of Notre Dame's second health care opportunity came in November 1960, when a plea for help came from Morehead, Kentucky, physician Dr. Louise Caudill, a Baptist, and her Catholic nurse Susie Halbleib. The answer to their plea came in 1961, when ground was broken for St. Claire Medical Center. Caudill and Halbleib are seen crossing a small wooden footbridge as they visit patients in the 1950s.

In 1980, a group of Notre Dame Sisters and Dr. Louise Caudill (center) celebrated the 17th anniversary of the St. Claire Medical Center in Morehead, Kentucky. When Dr. Caudill opened her first small clinic, there were no provisions for overnight patients. Mothers delivering babies were provided a few hours to recover before the mother and baby were sent home.

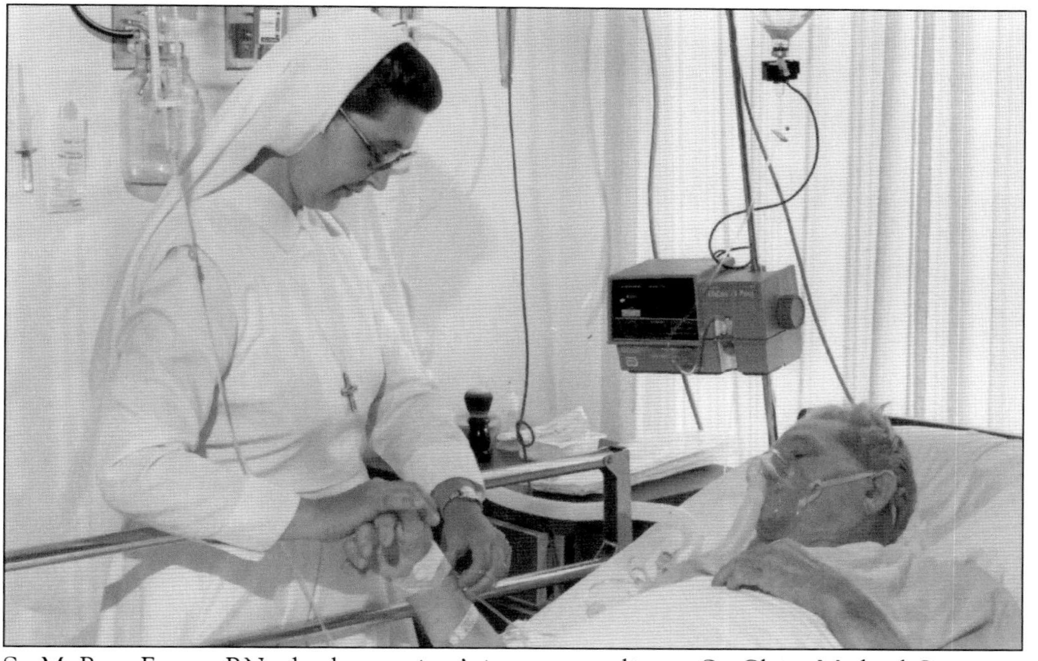

Sr. M. Rose Emma, RN, checks a patient's intravenous line at St. Claire Medical Center in Morehead, Kentucky. Today, the residents of Morehead and Rowan County receive state-of-the-art medical care because a plea for help was answered 50 years ago by the Sisters of Notre Dame.

Sr. M. Francis works with one of the young children at Redwood School in Fort Mitchell, Kentucky, in this c. 1970 photograph. Sister worked as an occupational therapist at the school from 1967 until 1973.

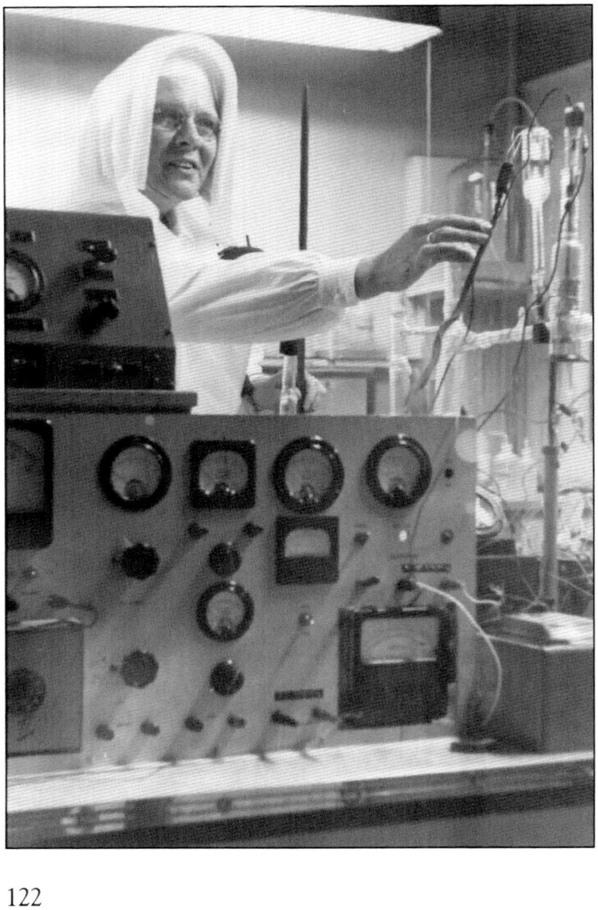

In 1935, the archbishop of Cincinnati, John T. McNicholas, founded the St. Thomas Institute. Covington-born Dr. George Sperti was appointed research leader of the institute. Sr. M. Julitta was a member of the medical research team of the institute.

Sr. M. Julitta is seen in this c. 1970 photograph from the St. Thomas Institute Research Lab in Cincinnati, Ohio. Sr. M. Julitta performed scientific studies in the area of cancer research. She was associated with the institute from 1966 until 1978.

Sr. M. Patrycia poses with two of the youngsters at Julie Learning Center at St. Joseph Heights. Sr. M. Patrycia is the director of the center and has over 46 years of experience working with children.

Sr. M. Carmella works with students at Julie Learning Center. She is a volunteer at the center and teaches Spanish to the children each week.

In 1995, the Sisters of the Covington Province embarked on their first foreign mission. Two sisters were sent to Uganda, East Africa, on a mission to assist the families of the region and to establish a school to educate the children. The school and convent are remotely located along the dirt road seen in this 1998 photograph. Shopping for food and other supplies entails a four-hour trip to Kampala by Jeep.

The Sisters of Notre Dame missionaries in Uganda, East Africa, are seen in this c. 2003 photograph. The sisters are, from left to right, (first row) Srs. M. Annete and Rita; (second row) Srs. Anita Marie, M. Janet, M. Bernarde, and M. Delrita; (third row) Srs. M. Paulynne and Jane Marie. Sr. M. Judith (Lucienne) was absent from photograph.

It was an exciting day in 1998 when this photograph of the first class of St. Julie School students was taken at the mission in Uganda, East Africa. The children were very proud and looked very studious in their new school uniforms. Enrollment for the first class totaled 39 students. Today, the primary and secondary schools have a combined sum of 395 students.

Sr. M. Delrita poses with a group of children at the convent in Uganda. Sr. M. Delrita and Sr. M. Janet were the first two sisters from the Covington Province to travel to the Uganda mission in 1995. They both remain in Uganda today.

In 2009, the Sisters of Notre Dame purchased the former headquarter building of the Salvation Army in downtown Covington. The newly renovated facility now serves as the home for the recently established Notre Dame Urban Education Center. (Courtesy of author.)

Sr. M. Reinette, the codirector (left), and Sr. M. Lynette, the executive director of the Notre Dame Urban Education Center (right), observe students working on a craft project during the center's after-school program. The center opened in 2010 and presently has an enrollment of approximately 40 students. (Courtesy of author.)

Sr. M. Kevan provides individual tutoring assistance to a young student at the Notre Dame Urban Education Center in Covington. The center provides students with after-school study opportunities, including one-on-one tutoring in math, reading, and study skills by community volunteers. (Courtesy of author.)